The Book of Johns

The Book of Johns

PERSIA MONIR

ISBN-13: 9780988629707
ISBN-10: 0988629704

Library of Congress Control Number: 2017962358
Persias Palace Videos LLC, Palm Beach Gardens, FL

Table of Contents

Preface

Our experiences and environments shape and mold us, build our characters, and with a bit of serendipity, bring us luck, happiness, and prosperity. When I was ten years old, I read a biography about a girl named Lotta Crabtree. She lived during the gold rush in 1848 and used to dance for miners in a saloon. The miners loved and adored Lotta and her performances. They would shower her with gold after her great performances. I longed to be Lotta Crabtree. In a way, I manifested my own destiny with this childhood fantasy.

My life has been one of peaks and valleys, a real rollercoaster ride. I believe the majority of people prefer a more even curve of expectations in their daily lives. Being the rolling stone I am, I prefer living on the edge, taking a walk on the wild side now and then, and then waiting to see what happens. I like to see what happens next.

I grew up in an upper-middle-class suburb complete with lots of friends my age, who all had similar parents. Our fathers were hardworking men, and most of the mothers were homemakers. The neighborhood was a special one. It seems that 98 percent of the families were the same ages of both parents and children. I had at least a hundred children to interact with. We stayed in this enclave-type environment until the neighborhood became more of a blue-collar area, and my family moved to the eastern part of Memphis, and we children began attending parochial schools.

Any dysfunction in my family was pretty normal stuff for the 1970s and 1980s—an alcoholic parent with the other parent trying to fix it. I was a typical teenager, experimenting with marijuana, acid, and alcohol. We all did. The nerds and geeks were far and few between, and besides, I was one of them. I was always the smartest girl in the class if not the entire school. Teachers perpetually yanked me out of class to tell me that I was too smart to be in that particular classroom. That was something I never got used to. I thought I was going to be in trouble for something I did, which is a sign of what messages I was receiving at home. Independent and hardheaded with dogged determination to have my way, I spent my time away from my parents' household at friends' or my boyfriend's house from the time I was fourteen years old, just using my house as a home base and a place to sleep.

At seventeen, I met in the theater the man whom I would marry. He was an excellent percussionist and as handsome as a Greek god. As a matter of fact, I used to call him Adonis. He had black, curly hair, green eyes like a cat, and full black eyebrows. His face looked perfectly chiseled, complete with a cleft chin. The body matched the face, and he was such a great athlete. Not only did he have brawn; he had the brains to match. The best part was that he truly adored me.

Unfortunately, alcoholism got the best of the marriage, and it started the downward spiral after the first five years. It didn't help that I was a crazed nymphomaniac, and he was practically frigid in the bedroom, only able to hang out in bed for about five minutes every day. What man doesn't want a blow job? The first man whom Persia married, that's who. He was just naïve or hung up from having a mother who preached about Jesus relentlessly.

My husband and I spent most of our time together, just a young, eager couple seeking the American dream and planning on living happily ever after. We purchased our second home when I was twenty-three and lived in Nashville, Tennessee, until 1988, when I decided to leave the marriage of ten years.

My ex-husband had such excellent genes, and I had always wanted his child. All I had to do was think the thought, and I became pregnant. Even the nurses I was working with in the recovery room at the time giggled and made fun of my decision to get pregnant and the immediate results. We have a beautiful son, who is the apple of my eye. I left the marriage in 1988, when he was ten months old, and moved to Florida when he was two-and-a-half years old. My ex-husband was devastated, angry, and punitive. He refused to pay child support, and we became entangled in legal battles until the child was eighteen years old.

It was not an easy time for my son and me. I worked long hours at the hospital and was fortunate enough to have good day-care experiences for him. Every moment was spent taking care of my son, working at the hospital, or diligently playing golf and working on my game.

I used to practice with an aspiring golf professional nightly at a local driving range. He saw that I had such a strong desire to play golf. He would stop and comment frequently, "You can't play the tour or reach your goals on a nurse's salary! You are a natural dancer and so sexy—go dance!" He would say it to me to the point of nagging.

Once in a while he would come over to my house and talk to me about the men's clubs and men's points of view and instruct me on choices of music if I ever did decide to dance. This man would give me dances and tell me how a stripper ought to move. To this day, the song "Shoop" reminds me of those moments together.

Finally, on January 31, 1994, I acquiesced to his badgering, drove to the east coast of Florida, and went to audition at Diamond Platinum. The short Italian general manager took one look at me asked if I had a driver's license and social security card. When I acknowledged the items required, he hired me on the spot without an audition. That was too easy! I was horrified when I saw a naked girl on stage and the beer delivery man just walked in and could see her! I wanted to go cover her up and collect a fee from him.

I opted to drive back to my mundane lifestyle in Ft. Myers. After another two weeks in my rut, I got the nerve to return to Ft. Lauderdale. This time the manager was a bull dyke in a tuxedo, who told me that I was too old for her club, but that maybe they would hire me at Royal

Gold down the street. I arrived to find the same Italian manager that I had met the first time!

The club had high energy and it was such a happy atmosphere. After I put on my leopard bustier and black stockings, the housemother informed me that at Royal Gold, they did not dance nude, but instead did "friction dances." After she explained this to me, I almost walked out of the club. The house mom minimized the fact of close contact and kept encouraging me to stay. She applied a latex covering to my nipples (something required to keep us legal), and off I went to dance.

My golf buddy had suggested I change my name to something else, like Haley or Brittany. I liked my given name, Karen, and if I was going to adopt a name for entertainment's sake, it was going to be very unusual. My girlfriend Jane and I had this discussion and one day she said, "Well, hell, you are Persian; why don't you be Persia?" We laughed at the obvious silliness of the name. The name stuck and fit me to a T! Persia was born in 1994 and lives to tell her story and share all her adventures.

After the first six months of lap dancing, not only did I notice a lift in my well-being, but my skin, hair, and face became smoother and shiny and had an overall healthier look. I glowed! I started believing that human touch might be the solution to aging. Do people ever really get touched or stroked enough? What a nice place the world would be if people were touched and rubbed daily. So many people go for weeks, months, or years without a hug. Hugging to me is a need like drinking water.

This book is a compilation of true stories. For those of you who lack a sense of humor, I hope these essays help you find yours. Read my book, laugh, and celebrate my freedom with me!

Foreword

As I pondered what to write to introduce you, the reader, to the auto-biography you currently hold in your hands, the lyrics to an eighties "Genesis" song, "Home by the Sea," come to mind: "Images of sorrow / pictures of delight / things that go to make up a life"—or something like this. Herein you will read about the sorrows, delights, the triumphs, and the tragedies that have gone to make up the life of the most extraordinary and I dare say beautiful (because she is) woman I have ever met.

We are, each of us, at birth a sky lacking much by the way of a constellation. Our heavens, should we be fortunate, shine with the primary stars of mother and father, perhaps a brother or sister and grandparents. As our lives progress, we populate our heavens with future stars: our friends, our acquaintances, and others we meet along the way. Some burn brightly, some burn enduringly, still others fleetingly. Some implode, snuff out, and become event horizons of loss, sorrow, or enmity. In this book, you will find some of each: a few saints, no end of sinners, and several very fucked-up pieces of work.

We read autobiographies for numerous reasons. Some of you will read this one for salacious interest—vicarious interest to see if they "made it." Happy motherfuckers will no doubt find their names have been changed. Whatever the reason you selected to read this book, I hope you will find something to relate to, something that validates you, something you will discover, take with you into your life that will give you a greater sense of self.

Returning to the metaphor of stars populating our personal constellations—the woman whose life is the story you are about to read has become the star that illuminates my heavens with the most radiant and brightest of lights. She is my soul mate. In point of fact, she is my soul, and I love her with absolute devotion. Many people have asked me how I can love so absolutely a woman who is not faithful to me, who does all these things you will read about shortly. While I can count the ways for which I love this extraordinary and singular woman, the simplest answer will suffice: I love her because she belongs to me with her heart, soul, and mind.

You see, physical possession does not love make. Love transcends physical boundaries and becomes something of pure spirit. When you love something, you set it free. If it returns to you, it is yours. If not, it never was. In loving this woman, I have learned the meaning of this axiom. How can one love what he cannot trust will return to him? He cannot love, because he has no faith. He covets. He fears. He confines thinking he can keep the object of his desire, but becomes only a resented jailer who controls a body, but never the heart, soul, or mind.

Home, as the saying goes, is where the heart is. Her heart and soul and mind return always to me, and mine remain always with her. This is how I love her and why I will always love her. She returns to me again and again. She is my image of delight. She is my life. She is the star that burns with oh-so-radiant brightness in my constellation.

Anonymous Admirer

Dedication

The names in this book have been changed to protect the guilty. I have complete compassion and gratitude to all the "Johns" who were thinking with their little head. I want to dedicate this book to my mother, Gloria, who stuck by me as a good mother would. Gloria would have preferred me to live my life differently than I chose to, but she listened to me, advised me, cried with me and stuck by me when nobody else was around.

Thank you, Mom, for your unconditional love.

Now this is a verse of a Persian nurse,

a delight in every way!

She will take time off to play the game of golf

practically every day,

Has the drive of a man—putt and chip, yes, she can—

but in Florida, not Iran!

One

PREMONITION

Three days a week I would load up my car and commute from Ft. Myers, Florida, across Alligator Alley to Ft. Lauderdale. Most mornings I was laughing out loud. The kind of fun I was having was something one would see in a movie. It was a fantasy come true. It was only my first week of work.

The anticipation and excitement of working at Royal Gold gave me butterflies. Once I arrived at the club and entered the dressing room, I felt as if I was home. The musty smell of stale alcohol from the night before, mixed with the girls' perfume and occasional cigarette smoke became a familiar and welcomed blend of aromas every day.

Dancing reminded me of when I was a little girl playing dress-up. It was so much *more* fun as an adult. I followed my friend's advice, who insisted I wear my nursing uniform in the club. Most girls wore long gowns, and it was required most of the time, but I started wearing my uniform every Friday, and it soon became a big hit. I even wore the nursing cap that I graduated in, replacing my navy-blue stripe with a red one. Oddly, I felt so clinical in the outfit. I think the cap, lab coat, and stethoscope were second nature, and I had no choice but to slip into the role. Never mind that I had on a slingshot G-string, white lace bra, exposed white thigh highs, each decorated with red garters. My red stilettos were a nice contrast to the white stockings.

Everybody loved Persia, the head nurse, as I used to call myself. I even had a red name tag made with the title "Head Nurse"! So when I really wanted to make money, I would opt to wear my nursing costume that day.

I danced from 12:00 p.m. to 7:00 p.m. about four days a week. Once the music started and the lights dimmed and changed to flashing, colored stage lights, it might as well have been midnight. I would slip into a fantasy world and forget all the reality I left back at the hospital as a real nurse monitoring and caring for patients whose next breath might be their last. No wonder men came to these bars. It was the perfect antidote for a stressful day. Poof! A little cocktail, a little lap dance, de-stressed, and back to work.

As Persia the Nurse, I had a purse full of cash. For a change, I could go to a nice restaurant without feeling guilty about spending too much money. I lived in the Oakland Park Motor Lodge across the street in room twenty-nine. After work I would go to my modest, dingy room and take a long, hot shower. I might go practice on the driving range for a while before eating Thai food at a family restaurant around the corner. It was a routine I became fond of.

After three days of being Nurse Persia, I would travel back across Alligator Alley to my other reality. I laughed all the way home and back. I guess that is where the phrase "laughing all the way to the bank" must have come from, because I was living proof of it. Stripping was the perfect job for me. Within six months, I would be living on the east coast of Florida.

It was so exciting having a double life. Only my golf buddy and my best friend knew about my trek across Alligator Alley almost every day. One of these mornings as I was cruising along, a little voice in my head kept flashing a message about someone arresting (dying) in the club or in a restaurant-type atmosphere.

The drive was monotonous, and I would push the thought down; it kept coming back, and then I began to think about someone possibly choking or having a heart attack. I screamed at myself saying, "Persia, you have been a nurse for so long that your subconscious mind has become morbid and negative." I pushed the thoughts away and looked forward to another fun day at my new job.

The day at the club started quietly. I stayed to myself as I always did.

In any work environment, I prefer to move around in a solo fashion. I noticed four or five girls at the back bar, indulging in champagne with a high-roller customer. The rest of the bar had a spattering of dancers and guests. With nobody to entertain at the moment, I decided to freshen up in the dressing room.

As I walked into the small, rectangular cubicle, I passed the long dressing table and made my way to my metal locker. One of the dancers, Queen Janine, as she called herself—a goth-looking chick, translucent alabaster complexion, deep-red-colored hair cut in a short bob, blood-red lips, and always wearing black leather. She had a flat affect and loved to gaze at people with that half-lid sultry, bitchy look. She was always indifferent, never smiling, as if the audience were there to worship her. I just loved to stare at her.

Queen Janine was puking in a tall garbage can, moaning, "Oh God! I feel like I am going to die!"

Only the house mom and I were in the dressing room with her. Ding dong! The light bulb lit up in my head. You see, from my nursing experiences, I learned that when people say they are going to die, they do every time. If a patient ever asked me to get the priest, I got the crash cart. Needless to say, I decided to stick around, and I moved in to take a closer look.

In seconds, Queen Janine fell to the floor with respiratory arrest. I cleaned her mouth and gave her breath. I instructed the house mom to call 911. Immediately, the dressing room was full of people. Vinny, the manager (a black belt in karate), was ready to jump on her chest and save her life. Adrenaline was racing through my veins, and I was frantically trying to remove the black-velvet choker from around her neck to feel her carotid pulse.

"Vinny, don't touch her chest. She has a pulse." Janine respiratory arrested four times before the paramedics arrived. I was buns up in the air taking her blood pressure with the sphygmomanometer I had in my locker. I told the paramedics to start D51/2NS with 20 mEq KCL and give her a half amp of Narcan. Balking and not sure of what to think of me, EMS carried Janine out on a stretcher, parting a sea of wailing strippers as they went. The club owner had arrived and rushed in thanking me profusely.

"What would you like? I will do anything for you," he spewed.

"Well, how about sponsoring me on a golf tour?" Long story short, the guy never even bought me a drink. The incident made the newspaper the next day. I had saved Janine's life. She was back to work the next week and very grateful and attentive to me.

The little voice in my subconscious mind had become more conscious over the years, and after this premonition, I listened even more closely. From that day forward, whenever anyone became sick or had a health problem, the DJ with his wonderful sense of humor would grab his microphone and announce, "Persia, stat to the dressing room!"

I might have seen paradise in a pair of eyes. I might have

felt fantasy on a pair of thighs.

I might have tasted honey from the hive—so alive! I might

have heard a single word, a sentence, a book, but I can-

not forget the smile that penetrates her look. I might ride

off on a horse at sunset, or I may never call her back. I

might wish upon another shooting star, or I might stay

on track.

Two

Tainted Jane

Some of the best times in the early years were spent with one of my coworkers, Tainted Jane. She was five foot seven, with dirty-blond hair cut in a short, butch-style fashion. This woman had bright green eyes that laughed when she smiled. She wore orange-colored lipstick on full lips that curled up into a smile most of the time. Her mouth was inviting, and I found myself not being able to take my eyes off her. Jane had a long torso but shorter arms and legs.

Once she told me that her grandfather was a dwarf and was surprised that I hadn't noticed those features in her body. Tainted Jane was quite beautiful, and men found her intoxicating and irresistible. I have yet to see a woman who could manipulate men and have them at her beck and call the way Jane could. I understood why once I slept with her.

Two things I rarely thought about before I became a stripper were my sexual orientation or my genitalia. Being in dressing rooms full of women day in and out expanded my thinking. Let me clarify the description of women. As a nurse, the groups of women I was surrounded by would discuss food and sex regularly. Stripper types and naked women in a dressing room have a different sort of bond. They are more open to talk about their bodies, which were on display for everyone. The conversation was more about which girl or guy they were fucking at the

6

present time. I believe that most of these women (about 99 percent) were victims of overt or covert incest.

Tainted Jane was in hot pursuit of me from the moment we met. She would flirt with me loudly in the dressing room and was always drawing attention to her pussy and the fact that she had huge pussy lips and wanted to surgically reduce them. I took the bait, and soon Jane and I were comparing the size of our pussy lips every day. The other dancers were a great audience for our flirtatious banter.

Tainted Jane insisted that we go to dinner with two other girls that we danced with in the first eight hours of meeting each other. We went to an upscale Thai restaurant down the street from the club. While we were eating our meal, she announced, "Well, don't you girls know that Persia and I are lovers?" My jaw fell open while she clasped my hand and was flashing me smiles. Surprised and disbelieving, the other girls appeared to be as stunned as I was.

I decided to take it all in fun. On the way home, Jane was driving in front of me in her Jeep. She kept checking herself in her rearview mirror and yelled back to me, "I need a new haircut!"

I yelled back against the wind, "Nooooo, I like my men with short hair."

She laughed and retorted, "If anyone is the man in this relationship, it is you!" I began to understand why men can't figure women out. They are so emotional and unpredictable. Being with Tainted Jane became a wild roller coaster of a ride. We spent every weekend together, going to garage sales or shopping at the mall. I wasn't used to having cash to spend, and it was so much fun having this new freedom. We worked five days a week and felt justified in our spending sprees on the weekends. It took some convincing by Jane for me to spend.

"Oh, Persia," she would moan. "You can afford that dress—just buy it." Some days our bags were so heavy that we had to drag them out of the mall.

Tainted Jane wanted to announce our relationship everywhere we went. She would constantly hold my hand in public, much to my embarrassment, and kiss me passionately when I let her. We had so much fun together. It was my first intimate experience with a beautiful woman as an adult. Tainted Jane was a wild, sexual creature in the bedroom. Very orally inclined without inhibitions, she could bring me to climax in seconds. Jane started to become jealous at work, and would interrupt my lap dances as if I were cheating on her.

Tainted Jane had many suitors at any given time. I didn't realize she was a hooker until near the end of our relationship. I thought men were showering her with gifts in exchange for her charm and beauty.

My education on the subject came suddenly one weekend, when one of these men and I were moving another garage sale purchase of furniture for her. We had loaded up the van and were on our way to her house; in our conversation, we realized that we were both fucking her. Ironically, years later this same man appeared and became one of the dearest people in my life.

Tainted Jane soon became involved with a man who had enough money to ruin everyone else's fun with her and take her away. He promised her the world and, in fact, left his wife and three children for Jane. That was the beginning of the end of my affair with her.

The real impasse Jane and I encountered were differences in our mothering ideals. Our differences turned into family arguments. Her son was a couple of years older than mine. When the boys would play together, my son would become hyperactive and combative. One afternoon as I was checking on the boys playing in my son's room, I found that Jane's son had all the stuffed animals hung in nooses dangling from the bunk beds. I beckoned Jane to witness her son's display of acting out.

When Tainted Jane saw his handiwork, she laughed and remarked, "Oh, Persia, that is perfectly normal behavior for young boys!" Needless to say, I quietly ended our relationship after that day, making excuses for several weeks before it faded into another memory.

Three

Doc

I think I might have been flat on my back, lying on the bar-side pedestal the first time I laid eyes on Doc. He was a lanky, thin man with soft, brown eyes and a weathered face much older than his forty-eight years. Doc slithered—almost skated—when he walked, moving quickly, with never a moment with his back to the door. Seven years in prison had conditioned him well.

My Mediterranean looks were the kind that made his knees weak. When Doc saw me, he knew I was atypical for a stripper and that I seemed out of place. Doc didn't drink alcohol; his medicine was marijuana. He loved the story about how I arrived at Royal Gold and my candid ways. The fact that I was a nurse and had quit to become a stripper was a reversal from what the usual dancer worked for. I met several girls who were dancing to pay for nursing school to take them away from the bar.

Doc had age, experience, money, and an affection for me. He soon became my mentor. He loved to flash his cash and immediately let it be known that I was his woman. Doc was loyal to a fault; he ogled me, snuggled me, called me a beautiful bitch, and even fed me grapes onstage.

I trust people wholeheartedly, and Doc realized that this naïve character flaw was not compatible with survival in this environment. Every day we would position ourselves in one of the four red semicircular booths, and Doc would teach and lecture me on this crazy business and lifestyle I had chosen. "Don't ever tell anybody your business, Dame," he would say in his North Carolina accent, "and never, never hook—this will defy you and destroy you if you do."

I gloated on our daily meetings. It was like having a lucky charm when a girl had a high-roller regular to visit her. As soon as he would arrive, the beautiful, blond, and very dumb waitress would grab me frantically from the dressing room. "Persia, Doc is here!" The house mom and gay makeup artist would echo, "Persia, hurry up! Doc is here." Their urgency was all about money. He paid me and the waitress well, and I was very generous with my club family.

Doc would fantasize about how rich I would become in this business and would say that the fact that I had brains put me in another league altogether. "You beautiful slut, I just know one day you will become a real-estate queen and own a small hotel down on the beach."

Doc came from a family of outlaws—nice ones. They never hurt anyone, but made their fortunes in weed. Doc had lots of grass and lots of cash. He also had his share of loss and tragedy that comes with illegal businesses.

As our relationship grew, he fell in love. He knew I was thriving in my new enterprise and that it wasn't an option to try to talk me out of it; instead, he worshiped me, stroked me, and encouraged me. Never in my life had I been given this kind of validation.

Doc was one of those men who loved large breasts to the point of obsession. He had purchased several sets for wives and girlfriends along the way. He urged me to get giant breasts, insisting that I would increase my capital instantly. By July, I was tired of talking and was ready for him to put his money where his mouth was. On July 27, 1994, Doc came through with his promise. "Here, Dame"—he often called me that—and with a serious look and his very southern accent, he handed me the money in a square block wrapped with red and green rubber bands. I ran to the dressing room, shaking with excitement.

"Oh my God, Mom!" I said to the housemother. "Doc just gave me five thousand dollars for a boob job!" The house mom and gay makeup artist screamed with excitement. The manager that day told me he would be glad to put it in the safe for me. No way was that going to happen; I knew he was a pool hustler, and I wasn't letting this much money out of my hands.

After Doc left the club, I couldn't work from being so excited and distracted. Doc told me that he loved me, and we planned to have dinner after I finished my shift. Within two weeks, Doc stopped coming to the club. Jealously overcame him, and he said that he wanted me all to himself. We started dining at our favorite restaurant, Café Max, nightly. We always sat in the same booth, and the staff was as happy to see Doc as the girls were at Royal Gold. He was just as flamboyant at Café Max with his money and showing me off, maybe more so than in the club.

I sensed that Doc wanted more from me. He would hint and suggest about us living together and tell me that I wouldn't need to work any longer. I would smile and placate him, keeping him hoping, not sure of what I really wanted. I was fond of Doc, but not in love.

I had made an appointment to have my breasts augmented in August. As luck would have it, my technician in the endoscopy unit I had just left had been an operating technician for thirty years and knew every idiosyncrasy of every surgeon in the hospital. I asked her who the best breast man was. She paused and cocked her head like the wise, old owl that she was and firmly said, "Dr. John." When I went for my consult, Dr. John handed me several lingerie catalogs and told me to choose a set of breasts that I liked. Hell, I thought, they are all smaller than my Cs now. I complained about the choices, and he handed me a *Playboy* magazine.

"There!" I exclaimed, spotting a naked, we, Native American girl. "I want big, heavy breasts like these."

I paid Tainted Jane to take care of me after the surgery at an island resort. "Jane, I want to eat shrimp, take Percocet, smoke cigarettes, and I want you to hold my head when I puke." She was a great friend and caretaker and did exactly as I had requested.

After the surgery, I cried at my changed body image. Jane loved my new chest. I called Dr. John, cursing him and telling him that I couldn't live with the new gargantuan boobs. He calmed me down, and I gradually adjusted to my 36DD boobs. Doc was happy and giggling like a schoolboy.

"Damn! We are going to the club to get your first dollar with those beauties!" Before I healed or could think about going back to work, we flounced into Solid Gold the following week. Braless and wearing a white mini-T-shirt dress, I immediately went to the dressing room to show all the girls. "Ooooooh, ahhhhh! Oh, Persia, they are so beautiful," said the Pamela Anderson–lookalike stripper. Another well-preserved blond cocaine whore turned about ten shades of green. She predictably enhanced her already augmented breasts to outdo mine the very next month. After obnoxiously showing off my new sex-toy breasts, I entered the main room and flashed them once at a patron, who eagerly placed a dollar between them. Doc and I left arm in arm, laughing loudly.

When Doc gave me the money for the boob job, I fleetingly had wanted to buy a new car, but in hindsight, my boobs are one of the best things that I ever did for myself. Not only were my breasts beautiful, my nipples were more sensitive, and for the first time, I felt like I had two new sex organs.

I never slept with Doc. He approached me bearing a diamond bracelet and a car with a proposal to live with him. I felt like the walls were closing in on me, and I practically ran out of the restaurant that night. Doc and I reunited six months later, but the romance we'd had was gone. I made an effort to have sex with him out of guilt, but it was a pathetic mercy fuck, and we both knew it. His past eventually came back to haunt him, and he vanished from Florida. I will always love him for his generosity. Thank you, Doc.

Four

The DJ

In the world of stripping, a DJ can make or break one's career. They all sound alike; all deep and dreamy with a perky happiness in their announcing. I learned quickly that they are all pimps too. Give a guy that likes to talk his own booth and a microphone and lots of pussy to order around, and he is one controlling, demanding guy who thinks he is Snoop Dogg.

The first DJ I met will always be my favorite one. I was clueless about the environment that I was working in. Coming from years at hospitals with schedules, policies, procedures, and protocols, selling my personality and dances in a bar was a job I couldn't have imagined. My best girlfriend at the time happened to have a thriving salon in Naples, Florida. She had owned several of her own businesses, so was somewhat of a marketing genius and had become my guru and mentor for my new venture as a stripper. She was a great listener and a great thinker. Most of the time I was on her last nerve with my impulsive goofiness. SPHOS was her nickname, standing for "subhuman piece of shit."

She could be a very nasty person to deal with if you got on her bad side; once you got to know her, however, you found out she was really a marshmallow to her core. When I had decided to be a stripper, I needed a name. At the time, I wasn't aware that a person was supposed to use her first pet's name and the first street she lived on…which means my stage name should be Peppy Paletine. That name would have suited me well. My golf buddy kept coming up with names like Haley or Ashley. Boring! Leave it to the SPHOS to say, "Hey, you're Persian. Why don't you just be Persia?" Naturally, I took her advice. It worked well in the club, and it stuck. Her next suggestion came within a few days. I was laughing my ass off, making cash and easy money.

"Whoa, whoa, whoa!" the SPHOS would say. "Hey, stupid, you are way too happy at work. Don't you know that people hate to see others in a good mood?" The old cliché "misery loves company" was true in the workplace. She would advise, "Never tell *anyone* how much money you make; and act like a miserable sad sack with all kinds of problems, and you will make lots of friends."

Well, that was one acting job I just couldn't pull off at the time. "Persia, the girls are going to hate you if you don't stop being so fucking happy! Look, they are women, right? They love chocolate. Next time you go to work, bring a big bag of M&Ms. They will adore you for a few days, and you can buy more time that way."

I followed her advice and had the girls all giddy, "Oh Persia, thank you, thank you, you are sooooo sweet!" they would croon over my gifts of chocolate.

My next assignment was the DJ. "What does the DJ look like?" SHPOS asked.

"Well, he is large, overweight, and he drinks lots of Crown Royal."

"Perfect! He is a fat man! Bring him large bags of Doritos every day."

The SHPOS was spot-on. The bags of Doritos and M&Ms worked better than hundred-dollar bills. The DJ was the only one who would try to match songs to my personality. I even had the nerve to dance to "The Stripper Song" when he played it. When the DJ was in a bad mood, he would threaten girls with playing one of the Monkees' songs if they didn't behave. I kept it a secret that I like the Monkees' music.

My DJ was soon to be replaced. He was constantly getting DUIs for pounding the Crown Royal all day long.

The SPHOS was always right about business decisions. My happy disposition soon failed me, and the girls complained often about what a slutty dancer I was. My run at the Royal Gold Club lasted about one year. I had always hoped that I would meet another obese DJ so that I could tip him with chips rather than dollars; however, it was a once-in-a-lifetime place in stripper history.

Picture for Persia

The fountain is a symbol of giving.

This painting celebrates the act of giving in its depiction of a fountain in a courtyard in St. Paul, on the Cote D'Abor, in France.

I can think of no better gift than this painting for my thanks.

When I was down, you took the time to give yourself, in order to give a person you did not even know a lift that was much needed.

Thanks for being my fountain and becoming my friend.

Five

REGULARS

Medicine and science were second nature for me. I grew up with parents in the field, and the subjects in school were easy to master. Dancing was also something I accomplished well at a young age, but in the bars, dancing was a sales job. Selling was new to me, but I was given the gift of gab, so talking was the opening of a sale. Smiling and eye contact were the closers. One thing that I did not expect to cultivate in this profession were long-standing relationships. Not only did I establish new acquaintances, but more than a handful bloomed into lifelong friends and colleagues who continue to survive the test of time.

Bars and restaurants have regulars, customers who come in daily or weekly. People are certainly creatures of habit. They always sit in the same spot and order the same drink at the same time, dance with the same girl, eat the same food, and arrive and leave at the same time. It is so predictable. Even the other regulars know the where others' seats are and respect their space.

Titty bars are places people go to escape. No questions and no strings attached. A place to bullshit and fantasize. A place that you can have an experience and then go back to your other world with your other routine and plug yourself back in after being recharged at the bar.

When I started at Royal Gold in the nineties, we were busy by 11:45 a.m. Men would come in on their lunch breaks. Most were business executives dressed in suits—groomed, perfumed, and handsome. A couple of regular suit-clad attorneys I befriended used to come to Royal Gold about three times a week. Both attorney Johns were yuppies with new families.

They would buy dances from a few girls and then leave for home after the rush-hour traffic had died down. Attorney #1 was tall, dark, and handsome, breathtakingly so. Any girl would be thrilled for a man like this to fall in love with her. He had perfect black hair and a perfect lean build. He was around six feet tall with round, piercing, sexy, dark eyes, the kind of eyes that one isn't sure if they are blue or brown. He had a square jaw and a pearly white smile. His voice was clear and deep, and his laugh was loud without reservation. This man was a great listener, very interested in others, and his composure was impeccable. Attorney John #1 preferred women of the Latin persuasion.

Attorney #2 was very blond and around five foot eight. He wore tan-colored suits most of the time and had a spiked haircut, round blue eyes, and a boyish face, the kind a girl or woman wants to pinch because he is irresistibly cute. Attorney John #2 also preferred darker meat on his women. He was crazy about me and became one of my regulars.

Within a year, I left Royal Gold, as it had become a hot spot for the cops to bust, since our new sheriff was in town, sucking the dick of the Presbyterian preacher down the street to get brownie points.

My next bar to work at was Stinkfinger. Both attorneys followed me to my workplace, as a loyal regular would do. I really was swept away by Attorney #1, but he soon became infatuated with a petite Puerto Rican brunette with the most voluptuous, delectable ass on the planet. Attorney #1 was an ass fiend like I never knew. He would wait for hours to get a dance with the nasty little Puerto Rican who was in big demand because she was fucking guys in the club. He stopped buying dances from me, but I used to sit at the bar with him for a few minutes, and we would lust after the Puerto Rican's ass together. It was a work of perfection! Little did I know that this relationship would take quite a twist a few years down the road.

In the meantime, Attorney #2 was still my regular and came to see me twice a week. I could practically set a clock to the time of his arrival and to the amount of money he would spend. One day I was out of sorts as I was caught passing a slow poke by a motorcycle cop as I drove my new black 5 series BMW. The car became a magnet for radar guns, so I guess it is true what they say about black and red cars being prime targets for tickets.

Attorney #2 was so sweet and helpful. He asked me to give him the ticket so that he could take care of it for me. I was delighted with this little perk and readily handed over the citation and continued my libation with my charming attorney regular. Well, cutie pie Attorney #2 gave the citation to his secretary, who filed it in Broward County. This would have been just fine except for the fact that I got the ticket in Palm Beach County. The situation turned into a cluster fuck. I was pulled over again the next month by a cop who was the double of Barney Fife on the *Andy Griffith Show*. I had taken a right turn on red in a school zone. Ole Barney threatened to take me to jail, as he said that I had a suspended license for not paying a ticket!

Thank God this cop had a partner with him whose heart I melted with my tears (a rare occurrence for me, by the way). In the past, I could have shown cleavage, pouted, batted my eyelashes with a puppy-dog look, but no matter what I did, I couldn't talk my way out of a ticket. When I returned home, I called Attorney #2 and pleaded my case. He supposedly had fixed the problem—not! I ended up having a clerk help me at the Palm Beach courthouse, who got me in week-long traffic school, four hours a night, to finally get my license back. Attorney #2 ran like a scared rabbit every time he saw me after that. His lame ass was on my blacklist, and our friendship became null and void.

Attorney #1 kept showing up and waiting on bubble-butt Jane; but she had a line of guys waiting on her, so he finally gave up and started on me again. We began plotting on how we could get her out of the club and fuck her together.

Leave it to Persia—mission accomplished. This girl had a piece of pussy like a filet mignon. Wow! She's still in the top five in Persia's history book! The first rendezvous was so good that we wanted a second chance at it. Every time we would set up an appointment with her after that, she would flake out on us. We both figured out that she was a pothead. She would show up again in the future, quite unexpectedly. In the meantime, our lust for her dwindled, and things changed at this bar too.

I moved around and had many workplaces and dancing experiences. Attorney #1 ended up becoming an endearing friend. He helped me with my ongoing custody battle with my ex-husband and gave me great unsolicited advice. Over the years we shared our personal experiences in life together on a regular basis. I never knew how much he loved my ass. It never even occurred to me that I had an ass anywhere in the league of Miss Bubble-Butt Puerto Rican. Man, was I mistaken! Attorney John #1 worships my ass to this day. He is my ass photo adviser, and as a matter of fact, some of the best photos on my website are ones that he has taken. Life is just full of wonderful surprises, isn't it?

Six

THE DUNKER

One thing that separates this environment from the rest is the liberty people feel like they have in dark bars with red lights and no windows. Most of the time if people go on a vacation, especially to exotic islands, it is an instant pass to drink and get naked, to lose all their inhibitions. The topless bars are convenient places for men and women to go and act out their perversions, and the decadent surroundings lend themselves to free behavior.

I was working late one day. The night shift attracts a bit of a different animal. The family men of the day shift have come and gone, and the night brings the perverts, young, broke boys, and the desperate single men who haven't a clue on how to get pussy.

I was bouncing around from client to client this night doing my usual smiley introduction. My habit was to keep moving if a gentleman hadn't bought a dance by the second song. I met a man from Orlando who didn't waste a moment of time. He was ready for a dance immediately. He was a large, bald guy wearing a tan sport coat and red tie. His shirt was disheveled, and his obesity caused him to break out in a sweat with the smallest effort of moving. The Royal Gold Club had four red, semicircular booths that were the most desirable places to give a lap dance. They were grabbed on a first-come, first-served basis, and there was no time limit once you had planted yourself in one.

I saw an opening and escorted my new customer to the booth. We ordered our beverages and he started making small talk.

"Persia, do you like to swim?" he asked.

I thought it was an unusual question but replied, "Well, yes, I love to swim, and I have been swimming since I was very young."

John asked, "Do you liked to be dunked when you are swimming?"

"Well, no, not particularly," I said.

"I really like to be dunked," John continued. "Could you pretend like you are dunking me while you give me a dance?"

"Well, okay, tell me exactly what you would like me to do," I replied, smiling to myself.

"It would be great if you could find another girl, a blonde who could help you, and you both could take turns dunking me," John said.

I found this request ridiculous and very amusing. I am not the judgmental type, so I thought, Whatever blows your skirt up, honey, as long as you're paying.

"All right, John, hold our spot, and I will try to find a girl." I ran around the room and found one of the wildest blond girls I knew and told her about his request.

"Are you crazy, Persia? I am not going to do some weird shit like that!"

I sighed and rolled my eyes. If she wouldn't do it, nobody else would have; she was the most extreme girl in the place. This was the nineties, when all the strippers thought they were supermodels. Fucking prima donna whores! I thought. I hurried back to the booth and told John that we were out of luck and that I would have to dunk him all by myself.

"Okay, I want you to put your arm around the back of my neck, then take your other hand and hold it over my nose and mouth. Hold it tight, and let me struggle. When I start really struggling, then let me come up for air." Hmmmm! This was going to look strange.

22

"Okay, John, let's give it a go." I grabbed him behind the neck, then I took my left hand and pinched his nose closed and covered his mouth. Jesus Christ, this guy was strong and very beefy. I felt like I was going to pull the muscles in my back! John was turning red, and I felt a raging hard-on in his pants. He started struggling and turning purple. I let him go, and he gasped for air. John had a big smile across his face and insisted that I do it again.

It just dawned on me that this guy was one of those characters who gets a nut from asphyxiation. I had heard about people dying from hanging themselves choking for the orgasm, but had never met anyone live and in color who was into it.

"C'mon, Persia, let's go again," John insisted. The GM started giving me the fisheye, so I had to watch his movements with each dunking episode. This was becoming very hard work. I was starting to sweat as much as the dunker John. I was still new to the club and the whole game. I dunked and dunked and dunked and forgot to count the songs. Fuck! At least he was a nice man and very grateful for the service I was providing. He didn't play dumb or try to stiff me.

Dances during that time were only $10 a song. We figured out that I had dunked him about $200 before the GM said it was drawing too much attention to our booth.

Dunker John could get a big hard-on only when I cut off his air supply. It was some kind of learning experience that day. I think of the dunker every time I go swimming. Later I thought that as a nurse I could have been liable if the bastard had passed out on me! What the fuck l was I thinking? One for the archives for sure.

I opened my browser, and what did I see? Persia's large

breasts were pointing at me!

A former nurse who kept you alive,

she's got game and plays off a five.

In Istanbul, East meets West, yet I prefer sweet Persia's

chest.

Her rounded nipples are open beggars. Her sensual

curves are Arabic stars.

Her full, dark eyes play enchanting sounds, while her

fertile smile the whole scene crowns.

Persia's Palace she rules alone, So kneel before her regal

throne.

Seven

MÉNAGE À TROIS

Threesomes. I wish I had kept a daily journal all of my life. It is important to write everything down. Even weekly would have been sufficient. I really would like to know how many threesomes and group sex that I have had. My first one was in my marriage, and the second one was with a perverted love, but those don't count in my life as Persia, so I will tell you about the first one that is imprinted on my brain.

Let's go back to Royal Gold, that wonderful, decadent environment I learned to love. It was just another normal day, and I was dancing for two Johns at once. They happened to be cousins. Both men were young and stacked. One was blond and the other brunette, both about five foot eight. This was new and unexplored territory for me. I was just laughing and frolicking all day long, playing dress-up, feeling beautiful, and being stroked by hundreds if not thousands of father figures that I never had.

These muscle-bound studs were a vision of delight for me. They were on vacation from somewhere in the Northeast and ready to romp and have some fun. These two Johns started in like so many men do: "Persia, please come home with us and spend the night!"

I was excited, shocked, and flattered. The three of us volleyed back and forth with the idea when I finally gave in and decided to go. Two strong men at the same time was a real turn-on that I wanted to experience.

When I finished working, they were waiting outside in their car like a couple of wolves. I followed them to their Ft. Lauderdale hotel. They offered me a glass of wine, and before I could take one sip, they were anxiously pulling at my clothes. Blond John wasn't wasting a moment! Very aggressive and the man in charge, he laid me down and jumped on top and started pumping away. He was rock hard and looking as if he was trying to impersonate a jackhammer! Cuz was more stunned than I was at his relative's zest for sex and was quietly kneeling next to my face with a flaccid member. I felt bad for the brunette John and insisted that Blondie give his cousin a turn.

He acknowledged my request, but brunette John was upstaged, emasculated, and deflated. He didn't need pussy, he needed a rock to crawl under! Blond John had enough dick for five men! Without guilt or compassion, he bumped his impotent cousin to the other side of the bed and proceeded to pound my pussy for another hour until I suggested wrapping the night up. Blond John begged me to stay. This was anticlimactic, and I was on my way out of the door, realizing that I still hadn't been with two guys!

A little later in my career, a customer and John I had befriended told me about a woman who wanted to meet me and had a special request. He gave me her phone number, and I curiously gave her a ring. She happened to be a touch therapist. As she explained, she helped people get in touch with their sexuality by teaching them the art of touching and massaging. I loved this theory and really liked meeting women who had open minds and were not afraid to be sexual.

She was married and wanted to give her husband a special birthday surprise—me, all wrapped up! I went to her office around eight on a Friday night. She had wrapping paper and a big bow. I undressed, and she started putting the decorative paper on my nude body. Once it was all taped in place, she put a big, red bow around my arms and legs and tied it directly under my breasts. We were both giggling in anticipation of her husband's reaction. Hubby arrived around nine o'clock. He walked in and saw me, and his jaw dropped.

"Happy birthday, sweetheart!" she exclaimed with glee. "I bought you a special birthday surprise!" They had obviously fantasized about having a threesome with the girl of his dreams, and I guess I matched the description of what he wanted. Oh boy, did I!

The Mrs. controlled all our movements as we all sat on a full-sized bed. We undressed her man together. He was dark, swarthy, hairy with a stiff seven-inch prick. He could not take his eyes off me. She insisted that he unwrap me. Reluctantly and carefully, he tore my bow and paper off my body. The wife started passionately kissing her husband. I decided it would be smarter to service her first, so I spread her legs and started eating her furry, dark pussy. She was a petite brunette with a cute face and was in decent physical shape.

After getting her nice and wet, I started to suck the husband's cock. He looked like a tortured man. By the look on his face, he wanted to throw his wife off the bed and fuck my brains out. All of sudden, this educated therapist appeared threatened and mounted her husband, kissing him passionately. He was desperately trying to focus on his wife but really wanted to play with the birthday gift she had bought him.

I leaned back and watched them fuck for about thirty minutes. Wifey wasn't going to have any part of hubby diving into my pussy. Like any smart wife in love, she wasn't going to share her husband. I left the tortured birthday boy and his therapist wife quietly, without drama, to their love nest.

Well, damn, another threesome gone wrong. Maybe it should be left a fantasy. It seems that people like the therapist think they have more sexual knowledge and can handle acting out their fantasies, but then they realize that they are not as free sexually as they thought.

I have yet another ménage à trois that stays in my memory. I was working at Stinkfinger at the time. A handsome, kind-of-redneck-type

John became one of my regulars and started coming in daily for a couple of months. It wasn't long before he began to share thoughts about his girlfriend and me getting it on with him. John had told me what a voracious, sexual appetite she had and that she liked her nipples twisted and sucked so hard that he felt like he was really going to hurt her.

Now, I had been in this business a couple of years and had been in enough situations that I really discouraged him from acting out his fantasy. He was persistent with me as time went on, since he knew that I was experienced. We then set it up.

One Friday night, we drove out to their farmhouse in the city of Sunrise. John brought me into the kitchen and spoke quietly, just in case she was listening. "Listen, I have her tied up and blindfolded in the bedroom like I told you she wanted. I want you to go in there and start eating her pussy and sucking her tits. Do this for about thirty minutes before you take off the blindfold. After you get her going, I will join in."

I was ready for action. I walked into the bedroom to see this very, petite, brick shit house of a redhead bound spread-eagle on the bed. Her hair was a deep red with a pageboy cut. She was blindfolded with a black satin sleeper. Her skin was translucent white. She had on a black lace bra and panties. Her body was very well proportioned, with shapely legs and cute, high-arched feet.

I told her hello and gave her a kiss on her very pink, full lips. Oh, she was so responsive! I started caressing her body and teasing her with my mouth through her bra and panties. John was sitting quietly in a straight-backed chair at the bedside. After teasing this little minx down to her ankles, I straddled her and pulled the cups of her bra down to expose her long, hard, pink nipples. I started to suck them with her begging me to suck harder.

"Bite them!" she moaned. I was twisting and biting so hard that I had to give John a knowing look about how right he was in telling me about her prior to our session. She wasn't thin or chubby but just the perfect size, with a curvy waist to match everything else. I pulled down her panties to expose a small patch of red pubic hair and a pudgy pussy with a very ample clitoris. No wonder the girl was so damn horny. I kissed all around her vulva softly like I like it and then gently worked my way up under the hood of her clit. She arched her back and was thoroughly enjoying the oral gratification. I probed her with one and two fingers, then fucked her fast with my tongue. I have a very long tongue and tried to make it feel like a small dick.

Miss Redhead was writhing all over her bed in her sexual glory. After about thirty minutes, I worked my way back up to her mouth, gave her a kiss, and looked at John for the okay to remove the blindfold. He nodded. I slowly removed the blindfold to peer into a pair of the greenest eyes I had ever seen with very dilated black pupils. I can tell you that at that moment, I was looking into the eyes of a lesbian.

John had unbuckled his pants and worked his way onto the bed. He started kissing his girlfriend and fondling my big breasts. One couldn't really tell that he existed in her mind. She kept reaching for my mouth with hers and was thrashing against the ropes and the bed. John untied her restraints one by one. She grabbed at my breasts and wrapped her legs around me.

In seconds, we were in a sixty-nine position with John lying there with half a hard-on. Miss Redhead wanted no interference from her man at the moment. He kind of stumbled around and was acting confused. I attempted to suck his dick a couple of times, only to be pulled away by the redheaded tart and have my hand shoved up her cunt.

She must have had three orgasms before I started to feel a little sorry for John. I thought to myself, that is what you get when you play with fire. Burn, motherfucker, burn! I politely excused myself to the bathroom and then bowed out of another threesome gone FUBAR! Is that all there is? I thought on the way home. It was amusing and educational, but threesomes weren't my favorite item on the sex menu. Next adventure, please.

This chapter would not be complete without mentioning one of my favorite sweethearts, Babydoll Jane, a long, lean brunette with thick, heavy, straight hair down to her ass. She had kind of an Asian look in the eyes and high cheekbones. The combination was perfect with her mane of hair (picture a tall Japanese woman). Her legs were long, shapely, and slender.

I always had hated my thighs because they were too big at the top. I coveted Babydoll Jane's thighs. Her legs were perfect for stockings, which she wore 99 percent of the time. In between those thighs was one of the fattest, biggest pussies I have ever seen. We used to giggle about it. Babydoll Jane used to say, "My pussy is so big that you could drive a truck into it." She had one of those effervescent laughs that was out of control once she started giggling.

She had a great sense of humor and was a heartless prick tease. Jane gloated in her torture of men. It was her style and her sport. When I worked at Royal Gold, this old, jealous coke whore came up to me one day and encouraged me to go talk to a John across the bar. She was always up to no good, and it was probably her way of keeping me away from a real money prospect. Knowing what a hustler I was, she had to steer her competition away as much as possible.

It was early in the day, so I went over to introduce myself to him. What a nerd! Short and blond, he had a thick mustache like a cop would have. He was wearing a suit and had beady eyes behind his wire-rimmed glasses. My first impression was that he was gay. When he spoke, he even had an effeminate tone to his voice. Not my type! He offered me a drink, and we exchanged introductions and the usual boring information about where we lived and blah, blah, blah!

I never asked gentlemen what their vocation was or about their marital status, so I had to be creative with my small talk. If they offered information about the job or personal relationships, then usually they had a problem to solve, and as Persia, I would go into my counselor mode. John immediately started talking about this hot secretary he knew (Babydoll Jane) and that he had gone out with her and was starting to have an affair with her. Of course, it came out that he was married to an Israeli witch of a woman who was giving him lots of grief at the present time. John was Jewish and therefore practical with his money in the club, but he did become a regular of mine. He liked brunettes, and enjoyed getting dances from me while obsessing on his new girlfriend.

As we got to know each other, John started toying around with the idea of a threesome. Surprise! Surprise! I would blow it off, not wanting to get into another disappointing three way; however, John's persistence started working on me, and we arranged a rendezvous one Friday night. John had separated from his wife, and he and Babydoll Jane had started living together in a contemporary, upscale apartment in Boca Raton, and they had invited me over.

John had told me that she wanted me to wear a short skirt and a black-stockings-and-garter-belt ensemble. I was a little nervous and naturally apprehensive when I was walking in to meet someone I felt like I already knew intimately, although we had never met!

I arrived and knock-knock-knocked on the door. Babydoll Jane opened it with her devilish smile and signature giggle that I soon became familiar with. We were in an instant lip lock for about five minutes. Wow! This girl kissed almost like I did. What a hottie! I was in love. John loved our instant chemistry.

We all advanced to the bedroom in a matter of minutes. Babydoll Jane and I left our garter belts and stockings on, and John was butt naked in seconds. He had a nice body and practically perfect penis— very clean, but just not my type. Something about him was so angry and gay! Jane treated him like some kind of toy to play with. Giggling, she encouraged me to suck his dick. We both played with him, but he was like added entertainment while the two of us got down and dirty. This chick was gonzo extreme!

It happened again. John ended up feeling left out, because he was. He became a little fussy and territorial with Jane, but I departed on a good note and feeling very laid! I had her pussy smell all over my face. Heaven scent!

John continued to come to the bar, but not as often, as his relation-ship became more serious with Babydoll Jane. They would entertain escorts frequently and would call me with one disappointing story after another. Every time they sent a skanky escort home, they would call me to relieve their sexual tensions.

Babydoll was curious about the stripper world and the bars. She was bored with her nine-to-five job, and John wasn't supporting her. I encouraged her to come work with me. John became increasingly threatened by my relationship with Jane, as he should have. I convinced her to become a stripper, and she landed a job at Golden Dolls in Ft. Lauderdale. She was a big hit and even sent customers to visit me at my bar. It was refreshing to have a girlfriend who was willing to help me and not steal from me as the typical stripper did. Babydoll Jane and I started sharing clients.

One memorable day, I invited her over to my new apartment with one of my favorite clients. He was so happy and laughing all the time. This John always brought champagne, chocolate-covered strawberries, and gifts. He loved to play with all kinds of women. Since he was an orthopedic surgeon, we used to have fun with him; when he would walk in the club, the DJ would play George Thorogood's "Bad to the Bone." It was hilarious!

When this John met Babydoll Jane, he was mesmerized like I had never seen. She was a woman who everybody went crazy for, and she knew it and reveled in her beauty and sexuality. This afternoon, John brought a strap-on dildo for the two of us. Babydoll Jane and I were over the moon about this, as neither of us had experienced a strap-on. Being the submissive that I am, I lay on my back and let her mount me first. It felt so good her fucking me and giggling the entire time, that I flipped over to take it doggie style, my favorite position. Jane could fuck damn good with a dick! We were very similar in our tastes and sexual routines. John didn't know whether to laugh or cry or which hole to put his prick in first, so he chose the first available hole, which happened to be Jane's bootie. Damn girl! She took his prick like a stick of butter. My asshole had always been an exit up to this point in my life, and I was not changing my mind about that. I was surprised and beholding when I saw Babydoll Jane's ass-fucking skills.

What a good girl. I thought John was going to blow snot bubbles out of his nose he was so excited! Finally—a threesome to enjoy! The magic ingredient was the fact that we were all detached from a serious relationship with one another, and it was pure, sexual, adult fun.

I really wanted Babydoll Jane to work with me, so I convinced her to come to my bar, Stinkfinger, and audition. She came to the day shift clad in her usual sexy black-stocking ensemble. Even though she had danced at another bar, she confessed to feeling nervous. Jane loved Icehouse beer and pounded about five of them before she got the nerve to go onstage. My drinking career was just starting; I would have been flat on my face and legless after that much beer. Jane brought down the house and had every swinging dick lined up for a dance after her debut onstage.

Stinkfinger had one rat-fink chick who was always whining to the manager about another dancer's dirty dance or crooked pasty on her nipple or some other thing that had made her face turn green. If I owned the club, I would have fired the cunt after the first sour-grapes remark! Anyway, after doing a few dances, Babydoll Jane came running up to me after leaving the dressing room. She was giggling her usual bubbly giggle and told me that she just got fired!

"What? What the hell happened?" I asked.

"I was doing some cocaine in the bathroom, and the blond tattooed dancer was spying on me and ran and told the manager. Hee, hee, hee!" she giggled—not the least bit concerned about losing the job so quickly. Jane really didn't care.

"I didn't know you did cocaine!" I exclaimed. She waved off the incident and bounced out of the door.

My adventures weren't through with my little trollop. The best was still yet to come. John and Babydoll Jane continued to call me, but less frequently as they became engaged to be married. Ho hum! I couldn't believe BabyDoll Jane was going to marry such a dorky guy! She could have had anyone. Her affection for him was real, but it appeared to definitely be a money-and-social-status issue for her rather than true love.

John also had two daughters, the oldest being a monster clone of her crazy mother. He would not have been my choice of mates, especially for a sexpot like this woman.

In the interim, Babydoll Jane was playing with one of our mutual customers, trying to nab him as a possible lifetime mate. He was her cocaine connection and much to my dismay, she had become quite a player and cocaine whore. My time with her was almost nonexistent now. I did have her over one day to meet another John, who happened to love tequila. The two of them were shooting tequila! She had her bag of cocaine, and we watched him pass out and sleep for six hours while she vacuumed the powder with her nose all day. It was boring!

Babydoll Jane and I went our separate ways and lived our lives as people do. I continued to dance five days a week, twelve to seven, and to experience new people and situations all the time. Jane maintained her hustle, and one day I received an invitation in the mail. John and Jane were going to be married.

There is always a certain sadness for me when a friend gets married. I was losing a friend. The wedding was at her mother's house in Vero Beach. It was a small, quaint ceremony with a big bash afterward at the Holiday Inn, where we all stayed. At the time I had an obese, hanger-on type boyfriend who just wouldn't go away who accompanied me to the wedding and ceremony. Even though he was fat, he could pick up pussy better and more efficiently than any man I have ever met.

The party at the house was fun, and a DJ was present for dancing. All the children were enjoying the dancing and music more than the adults. Babydoll Jane was her mischievous self. When the time came to cut the cake, she shoved a huge piece in John's mouth. She did it in a mean kind of way. I got the feeling she really hated him.

It was fun to be out of town at the wedding for the weekend. Fat John and I had just arrived in the room when there came a knock on our door. It was Babydoll Jane still in her wedding gown and grinning from ear to ear. "Come on and go out with me, Persia. John is sound asleep."

"What? On your wedding night?" I said with disbelief.

"Oh, I don't care. C'mon, let's go party!" Jane pleaded.

"Honey, I am going to hang out with Babydoll Jane for a while. I will be back a little later."

"Okay, sweetie!" Fat John agreed.

Babydoll Jane had her usual bag of tricks, and we snorted the next several hours away. My, where did the time go?

"Fuck! It is four o'clock in the morning, Jane! Listen, you have to go back to my room with me. I can't face Fat John by myself! He won't get mad if you are with me."

Jane had changed into a sleek, white Chantilly jersey dress that had an open back down to the crack of her ass. She was an absolutely stunning bride with a doofus groom snoring his wedding night away. We went back to the room to find Fat John awake, alert, sober, and puffed up, sitting in the room chair, glaring at us. We both giggled and flirted with him, sitting on his lap and begging him not to be mad at us.

He despised drugs of any kind and wouldn't tolerate being around them in the least. He knew we were roaring! On the other hand, he was so madly in love with me that he would have roped the moon for me if I'd asked him. We melted his frozen exterior within seconds. I grabbed his hand while I was pushing Jane onto our bed.

"Look, honey, I want to show you something!" I laughed. I started kissing Jane deeply, with his face right next to ours. His big, green eyes dilated with desire on his big, round baby face. His voice was just like Elvis Presley's, and I had him do his Elvis impression for Babydoll Jane. She loved it, and it melted the last bit of his icy mood. I pulled up her sexy gown and went down on her luscious, fat, hairy pussy—sweet like a white wedding rose!

"John, help me eat her," I demanded. It drove him crazy that I would share him. He was hopelessly in love with me and knew that I didn't love him, but kept hoping I would change. Well, despite his conviction and loyalty to me, he turned into king of the carpet munchers in about five seconds flat! Fat John made her cum like a rolling river. She started begging him to please fuck her. Babydoll Jane was as good a con woman actress as I had ever seen, but I believed that she really did want him to fuck her. The drugs had some influence on her mind at the moment of passion too. John became confused and upset that I didn't care if he fucked her, and on her wedding night. "I am not fucking a woman on her wedding night!" he yelled.

How fucking noble he was and what a fucking party pooper! Fat John made Jane cry crocodile tears of guilt. She ran into the bathroom, and I ran after her to console my sexy bride. "I can't believe he won't fuck me!" she cried.

Rejection never computes in the life of a woman as hot as BabyDoll Jane .

Well, the night was over, and it was back to reality that Fat John and I went the next day. Babydoll Jane bred with John quickly to consummate the wallet of her new husband. I attended the baby shower for her first son. She was just as gorgeous and seemed quite happy, but her cynicism had reached a new level. Maybe I just hadn't wanted to see it previously. At the end of the baby shower, she glanced at me with a smug, devilish grin like she was sitting on Fort Knox or something. I have been where she was sitting, and I do believe she had a good reason to smile!

Persia's Forest

Thick and full, like a forest of trees.

Warm and moist, like a summer breeze.

Wild and beautiful, the forest grows,

hiding its treasure—a perfect rose.

Eight

GEMOLOGIST

I met all kinds of people in the bars—people from all walks of life. John the gemologist had a shop in Ft. Lauderdale and would come in to decompress after work a couple of times a week. After our first couple of introductory dances, Gemologist John became one of my regulars and would dance only with me.

This was during the Royal Gold era, where the skinny, cocaine blonde dominated the night shift when the high rollers frequented the club. The more voluptuous brunette like me was put on the leftover day shift to work. The fact is, I never even wanted to stay up late and work nights. I had had enough of the night shift and of losing precious beauty sleep as a nurse. Those days were in my past. The day shift at a go-go bar was unbelievable to me! Wake up have my coffee and to work at 11:00 a.m. By 8:00 p.m., I was home with a purse full of cash.

Once Gemologist John and I got to know each other, we naturally shared our experiences about our lives as friends will and became more intimate with one another. John would come to the bar on occasion with some bride-to-be's wedding ring. All of these rings were huge diamond rocks, since he had a very high-end diamond store. He would tell me that we should christen her ring and then would let me wear it while

I danced for him. Heavy rocks on the hand do feel elegant. We would giggle when our time together had come to an end, and he would put the beautiful diamond back in its velvet box.

One day when Gemologist John came for his visit, I was bubbling with happiness. I had a new boyfriend I had met at the Royal Gold golf tournament.

He was tall, good looking, athletic, and successful. I was thrilled that he was in the golf business too, even though he was a salesman. He had a nice home and car, and our meeting each other seemed like perfect timing in our lives. My new beau had lost his mother to cancer when he was only twenty-three years old. I could tell it had devastated him. He did not have any siblings, and his only living relative was his father, whom he had become very close to in the face of his mother's passing.

Our relationship moved very fast (which is so typical of my flighty, Libra persona). I gasped with delight when my new guy placed his mother's ring on my finger. It was a lavender-bluish-colored gem about the size of a four-carat diamond. The stone was in a yellow-gold setting with two diamonds on either side. It was absolutely beautiful! His gift felt like a proposal of marriage because I knew how much his mother and her prized possession had meant to him. For this man to value me so much was the ultimate gift of trust and devotion. I couldn't wait to share my gem and new gift of love with Gemologist John!

The club was packed that afternoon. We managed to find an empty spot on one of the long, red couches on the upper level next to the center stage. I didn't like dancing in this area because it was surrounded by black lights. The black lights made people's eyes glow an eerie, empty blue color and turned their teeth yellow. I felt like I could never smile or be myself under the lights without looking like a possessed witch.

So anyway, I was all happy and bouncing up and down on Gemologist John with my new ring and making money as fast as he would let me. After a couple of dances, we broke for a beverage, then repeated the cycle. Most customers were worth forty dollars in the nineties. On a good day, Gemologist John was an eighty-dollar guy.

"Hey, Persia!" John said as he interrupted our dance. "I hate to be the bringer of bad news…but your new ring is glowing under the black light."

"So, what is the big deal about that? What does that mean?" I asked.

"The stone in that ring is not real. It is a fake!" Gemologist John explained. My new boyfriend's deceased mother had been ripped off. I felt deflated.

Gemologist John and I hugged and said our good-byes, and I left the club to go spend the night with my new Romeo. He had a sprawling house in east Boca. We went to his bedroom and then to shower together. The bathroom had a large, black Roman tub and a Swiss walk-in shower that could easily accommodate four adults. We were wet, naked, and excited as we started shampooing each other's hair. Being the naïve and honest woman I was, I couldn't help but tell him.

"John, I was dancing for my regular tonight, who has a high-end diamond store, and he noticed that the ring you had given me was glowing under the black light—which means it is not real; it is a fake."

"My mother's ring is not a fake! " he screamed with anger and humiliation. He grabbed the ring off my finger, and without his having to announce a breakup, I knew our time together had pretty much come to an end. Oops! I felt that maybe my candor had gotten the best of me once again.

Gemologist John and I laughed off the incident as another chapter in the life of a stripper.

In Royal Gold, we were allowed to do "friction" or "lap" dances, but we could not take off panties and had to cover our nipples with a latex coating. This defined us being clothed and not nude. Gemologist John was forever wanting to view my muff under my G-string. No, no, no! was always my answer. It was bad enough that I had gotten suspended for flashing my pussy to vice the second day I had worked at Royal Gold.

Like most men will be when they can't have something, Gemologist John became increasingly persistent to the point of begging to view my hairy bush. "Well, I have an idea, John. Diamond Platinum down the street has nude dancers. How about when I finish work, I will go there to audition, and you can watch and get to see me in the nude?"

He loved the idea, and I was excited to dance in the nude too! It was so naughty and hot to be stared at with no touching allowed—but kind of frustrating, to tell you the truth.

Diamond Platinum was one of our sister clubs, but we weren't allowed to dance interchangeably unless the manager needed girls for a shift. I had my day manager call and set up an audition at the other club when I finished working that day. Long gowns were required attire at the Diamond Platinum Club. If you wore a short cocktail dress, then stockings were required. No bikinis or sarongs could be worn like we did at Royal Gold.

When I finished my shift, I brought my black-and-gold satin cocktail dress. It had a black tulle petticoat underneath. I brought my black thigh-high stockings with six-inch black stilettos for the audition.

The GM at Platinum greeted me and told me to dress and then meet him at the corner stage by the front bar. It was a small, triangular, well-lit platform that I would be dancing on. I dressed and went out front.

I was kind of nervous about the audition. Where the hell was gem-toting John? I tried to stall until I could see him. The GM instructed me to dance the next three songs, taking my bottoms off only during the last one.

The atmosphere at Platinum was much more intimidating to me. Royal Gold had a dark, tin, low ceiling with dark wood, marble tables, oak bars, and red furniture with red colored lights throughout the bar. Diamond Platinum was all chrome, mirrors, black furniture, and purple lights all over the place with contemporary, angular staircases and PVC platforms. It was a cold, unfriendly atmosphere in comparison. I felt naked and chilly too, with the manager staring at me with a poker face and no familiar John to make eye contact with and the stares coming from the unknown patrons piercing my naked body like electric shocks. Where the hell was John? He had been begging to see my pussy and wasn't there.

The GM told me to dress and meet him at the front desk when my dance set was completed. He told me that I was too heavy to dance at Diamond Platinum, but if I lost ten pounds, to come back for another audition.

I was hurt and wanted to run and hide. Behind the GM I saw Gemologist John waving frantically. I thanked the GM and excused myself to go see my customer. John was out of breath, panting like a dog, asking me when I was to go up to audition.

"You just missed it!" I said with a crocodile tear running down my cheek.

"I just paid the cover and bought a drink. It cost me fifty dollars just to walk in the place! What happened? When do you start?" John asked.

"I don't! He told me I was too fat to work here!" I cried.

Gemologist John was as surprised as I was. I was the big money maker at Royal Gold. My self-esteem had been destroyed, and John had no solution. We both sat there, dumbfounded.

"C'mon, Persia, let's get out of here and go to the biker bar on the corner," John said.

I didn't know about this place, but it was on the southwest corner across the street from Platinum. I stormed out of the club with John's hand in mine, defiantly wearing my costume that I had auditioned in. Wearing a stage outfit was absolutely forbidden, but since I wasn't hired for the club, I was pretty much a patron like anyone else who entered. I felt like I had been punched in the stomach.

John and I entered this quaint little bar. It was definitely for bikers. Leather-clad Viking-looking men draped the bar. The place had a blazing fire in the fireplace and had the feel of a ski lodge—something one never saw in south Florida. I continued to blubber and feel sorry for myself with Gemologist John looking awkward as he tried to console me. We were used to escaping and having an exchange of foreplay and fantasy—not real-life situations. I came to the conclusion that my manager at Solid Gold had probably called Pure Platinum and told them not to hire me because I was his best girl.

Yeah! That was it! It hardly made me feel better, but it kept me from being totally depressed. Our dilemma of the moment then became the fact that Gemologist John had still not seen my very hairy bush. I was always given daily grief over the fact that I had a full bush and wore grandma panties. The new trend was a thin landing strip down the center of the vulva and thongs. The hairdresser had even bought me a special button to wear on my costume, which said, "Mary, Mary, quite contrary, shave that thing, it is so damn hairy!"

Everybody in the dressing room got a big laugh out of it, and I was proud to wear the button. I found over the years that hairy pussy never went out of style, and that the majority of men preferred it, but just kept quiet about it when the shaved look became the new trend.

Apathetic and swollen eyed, I suggested to Gemologist John, "Well, we could always go down to Thee Barbie House for an audition." I had never been there, but it *was* another sister club, and they danced nude on pedestals just like the dancers at Pure Platinum.

"Great idea!" John said.

It was almost 8:00 p.m. by now. Off we raced down Federal Highway to the corner of Atlantic Boulevard in Pompano Beach. Thee Barbie House was placed very ostentatiously on the corner of a shopping center in the city of Lighthouse Point called Shoppers Tavern.

Only in south Florida were topless bars on main strips with other establishments. Just before you arrived at Thee Barbie House, the Crazy Whorse, which was located about a quarter mile south of Thee Barbie House on the east side of Federal Highway, pulled you in with its large, mirrored facade and neon, naked girl on a horse.

Gemologist John and I entered Thee Barbie House to meet the Italian GM, Pat, who was tall and dark with a genuine wide smile. When I asked if I could audition, he told me that it was the night shift now and that I was too late. Our shoulders slumped with defeat once again.

Pat looked sympathetic.

"Pat, this is my customer John from Royal Gold. He has been wanting to see my bush for months. We were hoping to come here so that I could audition and he could see me naked," I pleaded.

"Okay, I tell you what. You can sit over in this section, and you can dance for him free of charge tonight," Pat said.

John and I couldn't believe our ears! Most managers acted like mobster thugs and didn't know how to accommodate anybody. Gemologist John and I let Pat escort us to a lavender room walled in glass blocks. It was our own champagne room, and we were all alone. I slowly stripped for John and teased him with my big, hairy muff for hours. Thee Barbie House became my favorite bar from that moment on.

Nine

Sex Talk

During the mid-nineties—the Royal Gold, Platinum, and Barbie House era—I met two psychiatrists in the bars whom I became close to in my personal life. The first of these was a large, hulking Jewish man. He loved women, like most men who go to topless bars. I liked the intellectual exchange with the shrinks, partially because I could flex my old nursing school muscles and because we exchanged notes on our theories of bars, sex, and the reasons people acted as they did in life. There really wasn't that much to figure out. I found that the guilt and shame in the United States on the subject of sex kind of spoils everyone's freedom of expression.

I really like when I meet a large Jewish man because most of them are typically very small. The big ones look like rabbis to me and are gentle giants who would never use their size to intimidate or bully like so many other ethnic peoples might.

My new John and I met almost daily in the club for many months. He would pop in on his lunch break, get a few dances, have some great conversation, then go back to the couch with his next patient.

One day Big John the Jew approached me and asked me if I would appear on a local TV talk show called *Sex Talk*. At this moment in time,

HBO had not discovered strippers yet, and pole dancing was far from being a class taught to the general public. Au contraire, my friends! Shame, shame and more shame if a woman dared to taunt a man with her naked body and be so brazen and unladylike.

The fact is that strippers and women like me who enjoy being sexual and uninhibited will probably never be accepted in most societies. I am in fact annoyed that it is discussed on television openly and advertised to younger people as a vocation. Sex is so much sexier when it is presented subtly and under the table.

I really loved the secrecy and naughtiness of the bars. I have no shame. Adult bars are for adults, not children, and ought to be in more private locations. It is a fact of life and should be treated as such.

When I first decided to move to the east coast of Florida from the graveyard west coast of Florida, my son (six years old at the time) and I were taking a cruise down US 1 so I could familiarize myself with the different towns. As I mentioned in the previous chapter, the Crazy Whorse Saloon was this eye-catching, peach-colored glass front on a building with large, neon flashing sign of a beautiful lady on a horse. My young son must have thought it was an amusement park. He screamed and pointed with glee. "Mommy, what is that place?"

"That is a nude cabaret," I answered in a very matter-of-fact tone.

"You mean there are ladies in there with their boobies out?" he asked in fervent anticipation.

"Yes," I calmly answered, while thinking, God, if he only knew that I had just started working at one of these places.

"Well, let's go!" he said anxiously—like, What are we waiting for? Are you crazy?

"Son, you have to be twenty-one to go to those places. They are for adults," I chuckled.

He accepted my answer with a moment of disappointment, and we continued our tour of south Florida.

Pardon my digression—back to my story.

So psychiatrist John asked me to think about appearing on this TV show. He also wanted another stripper with me, and the three of us were going to discuss with the TV host topless bars and the men and women who go to them.

John had asked the right girl to be on the show. Even though I was leading a double life, I have always been outspoken and righteous about my actions. I know the difference between right and wrong and just get plain pissed off over laws and rules that cross the boundaries of one's freedom of speech. A public forum was a perfect place for someone like me to vent. Now the challenge was finding another girl who didn't feel like she was compromising herself to appear publicly.

A light bulb lit up in my brain! I know, I thought—I will get Jane #2, my new girlfriend, to be with me. We had such a loving, sexual banter all the time we were together anyway. She would be perfect for the part!

I pleaded with Jane for about a week before I gave up. I didn't know her as well as I would in six months. She was being protective of her son at the time, and I understood that, but here she was the worst victim of incest I had ever come across. Her grandfather and father had both raped her from age four to about fourteen.

They used to bribe her with money to keep her mouth shut—but the worst crime in this nightmare is that the mother and grandmother knew about their criminal activities! The chills, revulsion, and anger stirred in me from her story just brought disgust to another level in my very being! Incest has more shame than people can begin to dissect, so I left her alone and decided to find another girl.

It happened when I least expected it. I was casually taking my time getting ready to work one morning in the dressing room and was talking about the upcoming show in the next week or two to anyone who was listening to me when one of the girls blurted out, "I will go on the show with you!"

Fantastic! I thought. This girl was the spitting image of Pamela Anderson—and was really, really, really stuck on herself too. She was one of those people who stopped to check herself in front of a mirror and then would hang out for five minutes staring at herself, primping, blowing herself kisses. She was just laughable and kind of nauseating. I couldn't have ordered a better counterpart for my personality.

When Big John the Jew came to see me the next day, I happily announced our new participant. We were thrilled, and then he started the ball rolling with the TV station in Ft. Lauderdale to book the date for our appearance.

TV stations are always small and underwhelming. I always had this glamorized fantasy of the big voice and the big set behind most television and radio shows, and it is really just a bunch of hoopla that very, talented people convey something big and desirable to the public. It took me many years to get over the "This is it?" notion every time I arrived to do a radio or TV spot. *Sex Talk* was one of those "This is it?" moments in my life.

I wasn't totally ready to expose myself at this point in my life. Let's face it, I enjoyed living my double life and secretly being an RN on one coast and slipping away to my sleazy hotel and being a stripper on the other coast part of the week. Thus I wore my new Cachet jacket-and-skirt-ensemble with a borrowed black leather hat with a large brim. My outfit was a snug, tailored black spandex and red leather jacket with alternating panels that zipped up the front. It was perfectly fitted to my torso, looking seamless, but I could lower the zipper and indulge the public with cleavage if I wanted to. The miniskirt was the same pattern, snug with alternating black spandex and red leather panels that zipped up the back. To complete the disguise, I donned a pair of blue, mirrored Revo sunglasses that Doc had so generously given me.

I felt like I looked like Jed Clampett on *The Beverly Hillbillies* with my silly hat on. Once I saw the show, I realized I looked pretty cool—as cool as Joe Cocker might have looked.

My girlfriend wore colors that suited her as well. She had a beautiful, soft, silky beige blouse tucked into some darker beige riding slacks and dark-brown calf-high boots. She also wore a light-colored hat but no sunglasses. Baywatch Jane (She could have been Pamela Anderson's double) had her luscious, bleach-blond hair curled and spilling over her shoulders down to her ass. It bounced up and down every time she swayed her curvaceous bottom. Big John the Jew, Jane, and I were ready to make our entrance for the live show. The producer escorted us in, then shoved Big John back into the green room and quickly locked the door. Big John's jaw dropped, and he barely got a sound out of his mouth before he was shut out. The producer of *Sex Talk* didn't want some boring psychiatrist on the show plugging his practice and theories. He wanted a couple of hot girls chatting about the deep, dark secrets of the Ft. Lauderdale titty bars.

Lights, camera, action! We were live and in color on *Sex Talk*. The set was so small that it was impossible to get nervous. Maybe they created small sets on purpose to keep laypeople from getting stage fright. Hiding behind my Revas kept me calm too. The producer started asking us questions about the men who came to the bars, our feelings about them, how they interacted with us…blah! blah! blah!

Baywatch Jane immersed herself into the fantasies of how men fell in love with strippers and how she loved the men and how glamorous and wonderful a life it was. Truth be known, she was a gold-digging ho and was as cutthroat and money grubbing as the stereotypical stripper could be. Every time she bumbled out a less-than-honest statement, I would come back with, "Bullshit! These men are normal guys coming to a place where they can escape and forget their stressful workday."

It was a debate made in heaven. We not only had totally opposing views on the bar scene, but she was fair, blue eyed, blond, and dumb, and I was dark skinned, brown eyed, brunette, and smart. The show was such a success that I believe they aired it several times.

Jane cared enough to record the show on her VCR. I never got a copy. We were paid forty dollars each for our appearance that night. The show, like so many shows, had a short life of about two years. The psychiatrist never got any press, but we had more adventures to share in our developing relationship.

Ten

SURROGATE SEX PARTNER

Big John the Jew and I were becoming good friends; it was always refreshing to have an intelligent conversation in a bar. The *Sex Talk* show was a huge success, and evidently they aired our episode several times before the station vanished like so many do. Big John considered me a very talented young woman. One day he approached me and asked if I would be interested in working part-time for him as a surrogate sex partner to his patients.

My gut reaction was hell no! I didn't want any part of being sucked back into my nursing profession. I was ready for a change and tired of the role for now. Once a nurse, always a nurse. I was a natural caretaker with sharp communication skills, and it was one of my many hats I slipped into smoothly with remarkable ease. An expert in rhetoric like a psychiatrist ought to be, Big John gradually hypnotized me into consenting to the offer.

I would make a hundred dollars a session. The patients were young males (twenties to mid-thirties) who had experienced erectile dysfunction after a few dates with the same female. They were not having sex with these women, but would mentally lose interest on some subconscious level or experience some kind of anxiety that would cause premature ejaculation or some kind of performance block.

My job was to gradually introduce them to sex with several sessions of foreplay before having intercourse. The case study was intriguing and much more interesting than drawing blood and spinning it in a centrifuge. My first patient came to my apartment around noon one day. We both had been instructed on the protocol. The first session was only ten minutes long. We introduced ourselves and made small talk and then we took turns touching each other's faces, arms, and bodies. We were to be fully clothed and stay free and clear from chest or genital areas. I would let him know when our time was up, and we would say our goodbyes until next week.

The second session was similar, except we would advance to the bedroom and lay supine next to one another. This session was twenty minutes long. It was extremely erotic knowing that no matter how turned on I or patient John had become, neither of us could undress or touch genitals. I discovered erogenous zones that I didn't know I had—one in particular was the anterior bend in my arm at my elbow. My neck and waist have always been very sensitive, but I was not aware of my arms getting my juices flowing until doing this surrogate sex role playing.

We were instructed to kiss each other on the lips softly, but no french kissing or tongue action yet. It was hot! I was excited during these sessions and was anticipating the next one as soon as this one was over. Predictably, the sessions would become more enticing and sexual. The third one, we undressed down to our underwear and were allowed to touch breasts and genitals through the clothing. It was also twenty minutes of erotic fun. Patient and surrogate were very careful to stay within the boundaries of the physician's instructions.

As I slowly brushed my hand over his cloth-covered cock, I felt his erection and so badly wanted to wrap my hand around the circumference of his penis. I have never been so aware of how the cloth of a man's jockey shorts were so ribbed. Patient John had sweaty palms and was breathing heavily as he softly and carefully felt my silk-covered vulva. John moved his hand down to touch my bare thighs and then caressed my long legs and feet with his hands.

On the fourth session, we were allowed to french kiss and instructed to use our mouths with fingers on each other's bodies. Patient John closed his eyes and gave me a long, lingering, wet kiss probing my mouth with his long tongue. I let him roll over on top of me and felt a raging hard-on in his underwear. Patient John worked his way down to my neck as he pulled my bra straps down and kissed my erect brown nipples. I thought I would orgasm when he put his mouth on my red satin panties. He kissed my thighs and legs and feet, leaving a long trail of saliva on each leg. I did the same to him, summoning all the self-control I had to not rip off his underwear and devour his cock down my throat. When the session was over, our underwear was soaked in pre-cum, and I felt lightheaded.

On the fifth session, patient John came over and as usual we sat on the sofa and talked briefly for about five minutes before advancing to the bedroom. We lay down fully dressed on the bed and started to kiss before very slowly undressing each other. This session was extended to forty minutes, and we were anticipating getting naked with each other. At this point, I did not see any erectile dysfunction with this patient. John was somewhat submissive and a bit timid at first, but once we started to kiss each other, he became very comfortable and appeared only a little nervous.

We both took our time, as the foreplay was extremely important part of these meetings. Hurried or rushed movements were the crippling factor in premature ejaculation or a limp dick. No problem for me. I was enjoying the controlled teasing factor of being John's surrogate sex mate. I worked my way down to his feet and started wrapping my tongue around his big toe while I gazed deeply into his blue eyes. John was kind of plain looking in features, but his body was hard, and he was very fit. John's penis was about six inches long and about and an inch and a half wide; more than adequate for my vagina.

After completely lathering his toes, I needed to let John have his turn before our session time was up. I lay on my back and let him caress my body. He had large hands and grabbed both of my breasts firmly while he worked his way down to my navel with his tongue. He slowly took his hands and slipped my lacy panties down to my ankles and fumbled them off my ankles and feet. My pussy was trim and smooth with my signature stripper landing strip of pubic hair down the middle of my mound. He covered my pussy with his entire mouth and sucked it in hard until I felt all the blood rush to my genitals and engorge my labia. He started to separate the labia minora with his tongue ever so softly and lick my salty juices out of my cunt. He propped himself up and pulled my lips apart as if he was going to dissect my pussy. My juices were running down my thighs. I didn't like the fact that I had to be in charge now and end the session. Flushed and overheated, we got dressed and said our good-byes. Next week was the most crucial session of the case study: we were to have intercourse and put patient John to the test.

The morning of the session, I took my shower and put on a very light layer of Calvin Klein Obsession body cream all over. I decided to wear a white lace bra-and-panty ensemble for our final session. Noon came and went. It was quarter past twelve, and no John. At one o'clock, I decided to call the doctor and tell him that the patient was a no-show.

"Dr. John, this is Persia. Patient John hasn't shown up yet for our session."

"I am not surprised. This is typical for these guys. They tend to have extreme anxiety about performance and intercourse and cannot stay in a relationship for any length of time. I have another patient to introduce to you next week," Big John said.

A tad disappointed, but ready to move forward, I accepted his conclusion to our experiment. I was a surrogate sex partner on three different occasions, and every patient was almost identical in personality. All three men were meek and submissive—and guess what? Not a one of them made it to the sixth session to fuck me. It made me wonder how many of these men were out there in the world. It was educational and aroused more than just my curiosity. Since I had to approach the men from a professional position, I concluded that from any other stance, I wouldn't come across men with this problem. As sexual as I am, it is a rare moment that I am going to wait six weeks before I have intercourse. What I began to learn as a stripper and aspiring courtesan was that premature ejaculation is prevalent and more common than not. No wonder people say, "That woman is angry because she isn't getting laid!" My sentiments exactly.

Eleven

BOAT RIDE

Strip club owners are all mobbed up. Arrogant and corrupt, they treat their employees like doormats. Whether they are actual owners or somebody's puppet, the same attitude prevails in all of them. Treat the women like cattle to keep them under control. Whoo whoo! Scary big-daddy pimp! The controller of Royal Gold in Ft. Lauderdale was no exception.

In the nineties, the entertainers frequently dressed in costumes—almost daily. Probably more than any other dancer, I just looked forward to our dress-up days. I had never outgrown my girlish fantasies of changing clothes and makeup to disguise my personality and become a different kind of woman. One Wednesday, our usual fantasy day, I decided to be a bride and dance to Billy Idol's "White Wedding" all day.

My hair was in an updo, and I wore a three-inch-wide pearl-and-rhinestone choker, shoulder-duster pearl earrings, and a white-lace bra-and-garter-belt set studded with pearls and champagne-colored sequins. On my head was a tulle veil that hung waist length so that my plump derriere was in clear view. My makeup had tones of pink, and my lips were extra shiny and full to pucker up and tease the men with. To complete my ensemble, I slipped on some long white-satin gloves, and now I felt as elegant as I ever had in my life.

I just happened to be featuring on the main stage when the owner or puppet man or whatever his title was came in to entertain an important client from Mexico. His entourage spread out stage left, sitting in the only champagne area in the club. The obese Mexican politician immediately demanded my attention. I spent the evening as his trophy. This was an amazing, eyewitness account of the most pathetic display of kissing ass to a star. The large Mexican was obviously very powerful. All those in the group, especially the strip-club owner/host, were tripping over themselves to light his cigarettes, getting him another glass of champagne or pushing me closer to his body. The Mexican was a light-skinned man. He was balding and had very large hands with sausage like fingers laden with several gold rings. He wore a casual linen beige sports shirt. His eyes were slits, and he kind of grunted when he spoke with a thick Spanish accent.

When my shift ended at the 1900 hour, I politely excused myself from the group. The club owner jumped up and grabbed my hand as if I were the queen of Mexico! I was amused watching the puppet man dance like a marionette. He whispered in my ear to be at the Doubletree Hotel at nine the next morning, as we were all going for a ride on his boat, or yacht, I should say. My new Mexican friend pulled me down next to him, insisting that I dine with him that night. I consented and was relishing my moment of royalty. The club owner suck ass started clapping his hands and ordering the waitresses over. I quickly changed from my bridal costume to my dinner dress, gloating while the other dancers were cooing over me and my conquest of the day. Fortunately, I had worn an evening gown to work that day as if I had planned on meeting the king of Mexico.

I dashed out of the dressing room to join the entourage (which included a couple of designers for Gianni Versace). We all piled into a black stretch limousine and went to dine at Yesterday's, a popular five-star restaurant around the corner on the intercoastal. The top of the restaurant, the Plum Room was the place to be. I had charmed Mr. Mexico into hanging on to my every movement. The meal was civilized and comfortable with good conversation and all of us enjoying ourselves. There were no antics or drunken whores hanging around.

The next morning, I arrived promptly at the hotel on Sunrise Boulevard. I forgot to mention that Mr. Mexico was accompanied by his "attorney," who stayed within close proximity to him at all times. He was a swarthy, black-haired, brown-eyed man in his late fifties. I couldn't figure out at times if he was trying to get closer to me or his boss.

The hotel valet hailed a cab for us, and the three of us piled in the backseat with me in the middle of the two men. The attorney started complaining to me that his heart was beating fast (he had learned the evening before that I was a registered nurse). He offered me his wrist and asked if I would check his pulse. Mr. Mexico groaned and whispered loud enough for his attorney to hear, "Persia, he is just flirting with you."

My brain changed gears to a clinical mode as I palpated his radial pulse at 118 beats per minute. We arrived at the Bahia Mar marina and hopped on the ninety-foot yacht. It was a magnificent boat with three master suites downstairs. The bar owner's girlfriend was present, and I became envious instantly. She was a perfect-looking blue-eyed blonde, slender with fabulous fake boobies. She was flitting around the boat as if she owned it—perhaps she did!

Mr. Mexico and the puppet man went to the top deck to sip cocktails and discuss politics. The attorney had latched onto me and we went to visit with each other on the lower deck. He continued to complain about his heart beating too fast. His color was normal, but he had a swarthy skin tone, so it was hard to tell. His skin was dry. Being the nurse that I am, I asked him if he was on any medication. He pulled out a pill bottle that contained a couple of cardiac medications like Procardia and Captopril and myriad odd-colored pills.

"Are you having any chest pressure or pain?" I asked, concerned.

"Yes, a little pain," he answered.

"Dull or sharp? Does it move down your arm?" I continued to examine.

"It is dull pressure in the middle of my chest," he concluded. I quickly pierced the end of the orange Procardia gel capsule and told him to open his mouth and lift his tongue while I squeezed the nitrate liquid out of the capsule. I hoped the sublingual medication would stop his chest pain.

Next, I called 911 and before you could say Jack Flash, an EMS helicopter was hovering over the boat and landing on the deck next to Mr. Mexico and the club owner, whose jaw gaped in disbelief. Nurse Goodbody, as he called me, had done it again. First, I had saved a stripper in one of his clubs, and next, I saved his colleague's attorney on his yacht. I wondered if he thought I was a jinx or a lifesaver in the face of this strange coincidence. Needless to say, our day of cruising and relaxation ended sooner than we had planned. The attorney went to Holy Cross Hospital and ended up with a normal EKG and cardiac enzymes.

Mr. Mexico took me back to his hotel for the day, with the club owner prodding me and taking me aside telling me, "Get him to take you shopping." At this point in my life, I didn't understand or relate to the gold-digger mentality of shopping with strangers. My shopping history had consisted of my mother and me buying bargain-basement pieces of clothing and then hiding them from my cheap father. It was a special day when I got a pair of new saddle oxfords, a necessary part of my cheerleader wardrobe.

So asking Mr. Mexico to take me shopping was foreign and out of the question. He already had worked that into our day after all, however. He obviously overheard the club owner and probably felt obligated to take me shopping. He took me to the Galleria mall next to the hotel to a swimsuit boutique. I chose a light-blue-and-white striped bikini with matching maxi dress coverup. It was a new type of fabric of woven cotton and spandex.

I wore it out feeling sleek, sexy, and nautical. I loved my new clothes! After a late lunch, we ended up in his hotel room. He started mauling me with slobbery, wet kisses then mounted me on his bed. "Ugh, ugh, ugh!" he moaned three times, then ejaculated into me. Satisfied, he went to the bathroom.

What a selfish pig, I thought. I was nothing more than a receptacle for his semen. Gross me out! As I sat there waiting for him, I noticed an odd gold earring on the nightstand. Well, just fuck me, and call it a love story, I thought. How many stripper girls did this fat pig go through a day?

I guess I had an epiphany at that moment. This was the beginning of my education into the real world. It was time for me to go now. Mr. Mexico and the club owner begged me to go to the Bahamas for the weekend, but I had a son to take care of, and for the time being, this party was over.

Twelve

THEE BARBIE HOUSE

There are some places one goes that leave such an impression that they stay with you in memory forever, like the Grand Canyon or Devil's Tower or the first time on a Caribbean island. Thee Barbie House in Fort Lauderdale was one of those places—pretty much the eighth wonder of the world for me.

At first sight, I marveled at the size of the building. It was a round structure built on the southwest corner of US 1 and Sample Road in the city of Lighthouse Pointe. It dominated the shopping center called Shoppers Haven. Only in Ft. Lauderdale in the eighties and nineties did you see strip clubs peppered along the highway next to high-traffic suburbs within the city. In most other cities, topless establishments were tucked away inside industrial parks or zoned in a downtown ghetto.

Thee Barbie House was the first club of its type, being an upscale gentlemen's club with Diamond Platinum and Royal Gold as sister clubs. They were all painted lavender (my favorite color) with pink neon lights bordering white stucco walls. The interior had chrome railings and lighting and pink and purple overstuffed chairs on purple carpets. Thee Barbie House had three bars, each on a different level. The main stage was runway style with lights and a champagne pit directly below with a large sitting area for high-roller clients to lounge. Also, the west wall of this champagne room was glass with showers behind it. A gentleman could pay a willing entertainer a hundred dollars to take a shower while he watched. Entertainers were required to dance nude on a pedestal three to four feet away from the client. Housemothers, hairdressers, and makeup artists were fully staffed on all shifts, and during those days, made as much or more than the entertainers. The dressing room was huge, with lighted mirrors, one hundred or so lockers, and even a tanning bed.

I was in awe of this atypical strip-club dressing room. Most club dressing rooms were the size of a broom closet with girls packed in like sardines. Not Thee Barbie House! It was the first room I had to get acclimated to. It was all so glamorous…the long, sequin-studded gowns, full stage makeup, and coiffed hairdos and pussies were all required protocol for girls working at this club. The DJs were all articulate, well dressed, and funny—not the whacked-out, tattooed headbangers of modern-day clubs. Professionalism was a contagion and conducive to deep-pocketed gentlemen who were glad to be teased and tortured into poverty for a day. I was literally walking around in slow motion in a circle with mouth agape as if I had fallen into a magical hole and arrived in a dreamland fantasy.

My first steps into the dressing room left me facing a nude, six-foot-tall blond bombshell sitting on the floor with her legs spread wide open in front of her. The door of her locker was open, and she was counting a two-foot-high pile of cash. What a sight to behold!

"Don't you have a bank to go to?" I asked.

She laughed and said, "Oh, I just made this today!" This was unbelievable to me, and I couldn't process this kind of information until years later. Cash had never been a part of my world until now, and I didn't understand it at all. My first night, there were only six girls working. I barely had time to slip into my black crepe rhinestone-studded gown. The bottom hem had a black boa that encircled my ankles. I had butterflies in my stomach when the DJ announced me. The contemporary atmosphere was cold and intimidating.

The runway stage seemed to be two miles long when I stepped out from behind the curtain separating the dressing room. I kind of expected flashing cameras to start clicking. I really felt like a supermodel!

After my three dances onstage were done, I hurried down to a drooling Puerto Rican man to grant him dances as he requested. At least I had had practice dancing for Gemologist John a couple of days prior and felt familiar with nude dancing now rather than my preferred "friction" dancing that we provided at the Royal Gold Club. I quickly got naked more out of personal preference and naïveté in contrast to a seasoned performer, who would bump and grind and then drop her dress at the end of the song in hopes to keep the client wanting more. I found that my eager attitude and free spirit worked as well as the hard-knocks hustler who fooled herself into thinking she got one over on some poor schmuck left sitting there with a raging hard-on.

As I spun around on the pedestal with my back to the client, I felt his tongue run up my ass crack all the way up my back. His tongue was wet and felt like it was three feet wide! My eyes must have been as wide as saucers as I spun around to face him. I was hardly able to catch my breath. He leered at me with a mischievous look. He was crass and rude, but I hardly cared. I gave him another dance anyway before I moved away from his creepy aura and let the night develop into something better.

On Friday nights, Thee Barbie House hired a live band that set up on the main stage to the right of the entertainer's entrance. They were appropriately called "Butt Naked". Thee Barbie House had a full kitchen that was open from 11:00 a.m. until 4:00 a.m. every day with every other day celebrating something and offering another food specialty. On one of their promotional days, Thee Barbie House had a picnic-style free lunch with hamburgers, fried chicken, three kinds of potato salad, desserts, and on and on. Free food certainly brought people into the club. It was like witnessing prisoners in a chow line. I had never seen anything like this! All these men had a resignation of acceptance about them; they were completely silent, not engaging in conversation with one another. It crossed my mind that if one woman was placed in the middle of all these men, the body language and behavior of the male species would change the dynamic instantaneously.

This night I was bouncing around in a black-lace negligee-type gown and stopped at a table at the foot of the main stage to dance for three men who were hailing me over. This was the night that I met John the Torch. I ended up dancing for him the rest of the night. He started in on how he had been watching me work the room. He told me that I had a special presence and talent. John went on to explain that he was a strip club owner and hired only female managers. Within the next two dances, John had offered me a job as a manager at his bar in the Midwest. The salary he quoted me was two hundred thousand a year plus perks. The offer was tempting, but I explained to John about my newfound liberation with dancing and that I was not about to give up my life in south Florida to move to the Midwest. John wanted to learn all about me. I told him how I was living a double life, working as an RN on the west coast of Florida half the week and then driving over to dance and live in the Oakland Park Motor Lodge the other half of the week.

"Persia, I have a condominium in Pompano that is empty right now. You can live in it rent free if you want," John offered. He was so eager that I didn't believe that he was going to give me a place to stay for nothing in return. "When you get off work, just follow me to my mother's condo down the street, and I will give you the key."

As the night went on, I began to like John and trust him. Club management always had a keen and cautious eye out for solicitation and prostitution. They want to keep the girls under their thumbs at all times. If an entertainer was caught leaving with a customer, it was instant termination of employment. Being the rascal that I have always been, I took the dare. I met John the Torch and his two friends outside at closing time. Just as I was getting in my car, the manager yelled out, "Persia! You are not to leave with clients!"

Fuck! How had he seen me? I'd waited until everyone in the parking lot was gone, and I left with the rest of the employees, as had been explained to me: Fortunately, I had given John my phone number, and he called me immediately. We agreed to meet at his mother's place at ten the next morning.

Part of me still thought he was bullshitting, but I arrived punctually at ten sharp. It was awkward to meet John in the daytime at his mother's house, away from the smoky, lavender-and-chrome ambiance of Thee Barbie House. John was good for his word and handed me a set of keys to the duplex on Riverside Drive. We both said good-bye to Mom, and I followed him over to the apartment, which was about a mile away. It was a four-room unit that I could tell had not been lived in for a while. The walls were lined in silvery foil wallpaper and had the seventies furniture and light fixtures to match.

Retro Florida-style beach living—I loved it! The bedroom had twin beds with quilted bedspreads with a sunflower pattern on them. The north wall had a tall, six-drawer dresser. The kitchen was the only room I rarely went in. It had a tiny, dirty stove with cockroach carcasses everywhere. It gave me shivers up and down my spine. You see one cockroach and there are five hundred somewhere; if you see two, then there are about twenty-five hundred in the walls.

John the Torch had to get back to his Midwest stomping grounds, so he left, and I was in my new, rent-free apartment—wow! That was easy. This was a great situation.

That day I started my new routine. First, I decided to stop working as a nurse and moved over to the east coast permanently within the month. Every morning, before going to work at Royal Gold, I would wake up and go to Café Sportivo on Atlantic Boulevard for a cappuccino and tiramisu and a visit with shop owner, Anna, a large Italian woman: I discovered that an espresso buzz and the sugar from the delicious pastry were a perfect injection of caffeine and sugar conducive for making money. This was my breakfast of champions! After my eight-hour shift at Royal Gold, I would drive five minutes back to my waterside apartment (the intracoastal was my front yard and the Atlantic Ocean was a block over and my backyard), take a shower and a one-hour nap and then dance the night shift at Thee Barbie House. I danced double shifts every day through the summer of 1994 and quickly recovered from my $15,000 credit-card debt. I was elated and exhausted simultaneously.

In all of the bars I have worked in, certain characters always leave lasting impressions, especially women with remarkable beauty. It goes without saying that gorgeous women are a necessary ingredient in the success of a topless bar. It was a relief to work with the most beautiful women, even if they were my competition. The bar was a busier, happier place if the staff was beautiful.

One dancer I noticed at Thee Barbie House was a stunning redhead. She had a thick, deep-red mane of wavy and luscious hair. Her skin was pink and creamy, she had light, hazel eyes, and her figure was voluptuous and perfectly proportioned.

I found myself staring at her to the point of distraction. It was like dancing in the company of an Ann Margret look alike. We saw each other only in passing between onstage dance rotations. I wish I had taken my time to become closer to her and develop a friendship.

Another coworker who became an endearing acquaintance was a blonde waitress, an older gal in her forties. She was a happy-go-lucky hippie chick, classic long, straight, dishwater-blonde hair, no makeup, and just a little mascara. She wasn't competitive with the other females in the club (against the norm) and was forever talking about the next pet she was planning to rescue.

Once I needed a ride back to my apartment, and she was happy to offer me one. There was one obstacle: all her doors were jammed shut, and I had to climb through the sunroof to get into the car, and then I landed ass first on a fifty-pound bag of open dog food.

John the Torch was spending quite of bit of his time in Florida these days. I learned from his own admission that he used to be a pimp. Because of his history, he expressed to me that he was adamantly against dancers hooking. I never asked him why directly, but I arrived at my answer to this question several years later.

In the meantime, John was attempting to mentor me. He was short in stature, blond, blue eyed, and square jawed, with beautiful features. John the Torch was strikingly handsome. He never once made a pass at me; his motives were not sexual, but business related. John liked to see people succeed and had many who worshiped him because he had helped them in business.

John had employed a man from Australia to run one of his businesses. He accompanied us to a sweatshop in Coconut Grove. His friend—employee or whatever he was—was a large Aussie dude who was profusely expressed his undying gratitude about John's assistance in his life. They were so friendly, and I was impressed at their bond. My gut told me, however, that John the Torch owned the people he hired. We were on our way to meet a clothing designer in the Grove. John had also helped him get his business started.

We entered the upper room, where about twenty women were sewing furiously on the machines, putting designer gowns together. John had me try on and model every style and every outfit. He was fitting me in a wardrobe to dance and also to wear to functions, insisting that I take whatever garments I wanted. I felt uncomfortable and not sure about the polite or correct thing to do. I had never been in this kind of situation in my life. He was generous and persistent, and after about three hours, we left with a cartful of clothing worth thousands of dollars. The fabrics were soft, durable, and very high quality. Many of the dresses were decorated with hand-strung beads.

I was puzzled and was trying to figure out John's angle here. I knew he wanted something from me, and his generosity had a purpose behind it, but I hadn't figured it out yet. The designer had a similar demeanor to that of the Aussie, bragging about all John had done for him, giving him all the credit for the fame and fortune he had acquired, which was ample.

After we left the sweatshop, we went to the designer's home in the Grove. It was a Spanish-style home, very quaint and well decorated. His wife had prepared a lovely meal for us. I felt like I was with one big, happy family. The Aussie and the dressmaker continually expressed their gratitude to John as if they were both indebted sons of a king.

After dinner, John took me to the Aussie's store in the Grove, where he sold leather goods, bathing suits, and shoes. John insisted that I try on a stripper bathing suit that had an American-flag pattern, and he started taking photos of me as I posed. The day had come to an end, and John took me home. John would return in a couple of weeks.

On his next trip, John was determined to teach me how to "hustle" clients in the club. I really didn't like this idea. I am honest to a fault, I guess, and any kind of deception just doesn't feel natural. He might have been a retired pimp, but it was a muscle he had flexed many times.

My innocence seemed to bring to the surface an uncontrollable urge in him to mold a young woman and bring her into his world. I was embarrassed for him when he showed up at Royal Gold one day to visit because had parked his Excalibur in the front by the valet and he walked in wearing a long fur coat. He certainly dressed the part of a pimp, and his appearance made me uncomfortable.

John the Torch was there to hang out, watch me, and give me a lesson in hustling. I had met an older, portly gentleman that day who had become infatuated with me; John pulled me over and excitedly suggested that I get him to take me shopping the next day. "Get him to meet you at your hotel. Do not ride with him! You must take control of the situation and insist on driving. Dress to the nines with the shortest skirt you have and the highest stiletto heels. Play on his emotions by taking him to a sports store and buying everything for your son. Next, take him to Cartier and clean up. Save all the receipts for the merchandise, return the items the next day, and keep the cash. I will be just a few feet behind you all the way, following you to make sure you are safe."

Oh no! This was not me at all. An act of deception like this was so foreign to me. John was so eager to teach me, and he had given me all those beautiful clothes. Feeling obligated, I agreed to do the dirty deeds. I set the rendezvous up with the large man to meet at the hotel across the street from Solid Gold. I saw my prey arrive punctually at 10:00 a.m.

He offered to drive, but I insisted that I drive (as John the Torch had instructed me), and I proceeded to stuff his fat ass in the passenger side of my tiny Toyota Paseo. We started heading down Federal Highway, our destination the Boca Town Center mall for our shopping spree. It was a muggy, cloudy day with a light drizzle coming down. In my rear-view mirror, I could see John in his white Mercedes Benz. John being my tagalong chaperone was making an already uncomfortable situation more difficult. Even his driving style was mischievous, darting in and out of traffic and sneaking up on us. I could feel his body language like a strong vibration coming from his automobile. It was strange knowing that we were being followed and that my victim had no clue.

We arrived at the mall entrance ready to enter. John had given me specific instructions about every detail, including how I should dress for the occasion. All my life I have been stared at in public, so I always made an effort to dress down or more on the conservative side. Now look at me! Here I was, a statuesque brunette dressed in a black suit with large brass buttons. The skirt was up to my pussy, and I wore seven-inch patent-leather high heels, a combination that showed off my long legs. The jacket of my suit was midriff baring, where you could see an inch of skin, and the sleeves were long and cuffed. It was early and not appropriate attire for the middle of the day. I felt like a streetwalker, with a thousand eyes piercing my flesh as I walked alongside an obvious mismatch of a shopping partner. Thank God in heaven the first store to the right was Champs. I could feel John's presence looming behind me, and I caught a glimpse of him smiling from ear to ear. I knew he was getting an adrenaline rush out of the moment, while I was overwhelmed with humiliation and wanted this unnatural act to come to an end. The fat man agreed to all of my purchases: soccer balls, tennis shoes, Umbro shorts, shirts, and hats that tallied up to $300 before we left the store.

Cartier was a short walk, but the fat man was already becoming uneasy with the idea of further shopping. My heart was not in it either, so when the fat man suggested that we go to lunch, I gladly consented. I felt John's presence behind me and sensed his frustration when we left the entrance of Cartier and walked to the mall's exit. He looked as if he was going to throw his hands up in the air. For lunch we went to the fat man's favorite barbecue place in Florida. I became annoyed with his cheap taste and lack of elegance as we sat there. This date couldn't end soon enough for me! Back at the hotel, we said our thank you's and good-byes, and then John and I took a ride in the Mercedes to discuss the event. John was beaming and had an almost-villainous grin. He was expressing how proud he was of my first hustle.

I couldn't wait to get out of my slutty costume and become my real self again. Between John's long fur coat and his underlying hunger to use me in some way, I became mistrustful and unwilling with him.

A couple of weeks later, John presented an offer to me.

"Persia, look, I would like to open up a shoe store in Pompano Beach. Very soon all the dancers are going to stop wearing stilettos and only wear platform shoes to dance."

Inwardly, I balked at the idea and thought back to the seventies, when platforms were all women and girls were wearing. I told myself that wasn't coming back. Years later—and not many years—I realized that John the Torch was a man of vision and had been spot-on. I had refused his offer and the opportunity of a lifetime. The admiration and loyalty of the dressmaker and Aussie shop owner were validated by their profits and success. My innocence was revealed as ignorance when I eventually realized my mistake.

I saw John the Torch only one more time after that. I was telling him about a client from the club with whom I had been golfing, dining, and shopping recently. I thought he would be pleased at my new conquest, but as I explained the relationship, his jaw became tight, and he expressed that this was the kind of fraternizing that was on the fringes of prostitution. He shunned me, and his mixed messages about hustling had left me confused.

Shortly after that, my days of Royal Gold, Diamond Platinum, and Thee Barbie House would come to an end. One day, Cocaine Jane, toxic with envy, ran to the GM, screaming about an imaginary hand job

I was giving a customer. She succeeded in having me fired, but her bad attitude also got her fired as well. This chapter in my life was over, so I left the duplex John had given me and headed west to Coral Springs to work at yet another sister club, Stinkfinger.

In the years to follow, the residents of Lighthouse Pointe complained bitterly about Thee Barbie House in the middle of the main shopping center in their community. Eventually, the citizens convinced the local government to demolish the building. It was a sad day in my life. I drove to the site and mourned the heap of concrete rubble while explaining to my small son what a monument it once had been.

Those times were the greatest memories of my life. Away with the rubble went the runway stages for strippers, the elegant ball gowns, the makeup artists, the C-notes flying in the air every night, the champagne flowing, the naked girls taking public showers behind glass walls, my quaint duplex, John the Torch, and my dream of success. As we sat in the car, it reminded me of the line from Joni Mitchell's song: "And they paved paradise and putting up a parking lot, ooh yeah, yeah, yeah!" A year later, Thee Barbie House became a Walgreens. Progress can be a sad thing.

Thirteen

JUNGLE BUNNY

She was just under six feet tall, with short, dark, red hair, perfectly straight teeth, and a sparkling smile to match her lilting, contagious laugh. Her eyes, as blue as the Caribbean Sea, danced with mischief. That was my girl Ginger Jane. I am all about work when I am working; I am focused and relentless. Even though I am an extrovert, I am usually shy when first meeting people and usually put up resistance against getting involved or getting to know someone, Ginger Jane included. Any woman I have ever become involved with always approached me, unsolicited and aggressively. I usually resisted their efforts at first.

Silly me, I want to believe there are women who just naturally love me and want a real friendship. Even members of my own sex have ulterior motives and personal agendas. In the clubs, I have undying energy to dance and a drive to make money, which always piqued the interest of my peers from the start. The memories I have with Ginger Jane have given me hours of laughter in real time and in my memory bank; they are with the kind that makes you laugh out loud with joy!

This Ginger Jane taught me two things: what a best friend could be and that redheaded people are evil and truly have ice in their veins. Ginger Jane was athletic, vivacious, horny, demure, jealous of the world, and like most Canadians, had a huge chip on her shoulder. She had no reservations when it came to gossiping, telling a good joke, laughing with the group, or moaning with blue eyes rolling back while receiving great physical pleasure during her lap dances. I wish digital cameras had not been so expensive during the nineties, because I would have had thousands of photos of this gorgeous woman; instead, I have a handful of Polaroids.

Ginger Jane was a Persia admirer and worshiper. My dysfunctional wiring seems to attract women that way—not for healthy, "normal" friendships. Since I revel in the attention, the dysfunction always worked for me. Ginger Jane was no exception, and our fantasy work environment was fuel to the fire.

Ginger Jane had a B cup bra size but was a big-boob hound. Maybe because of her smaller chest size, she coveted larger-breasted women. I was blessed with perfectly round, perky C cups by the time I was thirteen, and my new breast augmentation was a DD version of the perfect breasts. They were big, heavy, soft, pendulous boobies, a sight to behold and a delight to touch. When I was younger, I was so frustrated that I could not pass the pencil test (holding a pencil in place underneath each boob). Now that I had my gigantic DDs, I could hold a box of pencils under each breast if I wanted to.

When Ginger Jane and I became friends, we used to give each other lap dances before the club would open. She was grabbing, jiggling, slapping, and sucking on my breasts every chance she got. Ginger Jane was forever seeking me out to do double dances or impress an apprehensive customer in hopes that if he liked her friend's boobs, maybe she could finagle a dance or two out of the connection.

At least once a month the local titty bars would have costume day for the entertainers. Clubs were always promoting the girls during football games (Jersey Day) or capitalizing on some kind of holiday theme or gimmick to add a little spice to the mundane routine of our world. I have a great photo of Ginger Jane and me in the dressing room on this particular costume day. Without knowing it, we both chose to be

Playboy Bunnies. Ginger Jane wore a hot, red bunny suit with a tail with red patent stilettos to match. I wore the classic, traditional Playboy Bunny black bustier, satin white bow tie, and black stockings with high heels. I also had a bunny tail and ears, but my ears were huge, and I looked more like a jackrabbit! When I stepped onto the main stage to do my feature dance in my costume, I felt far from sexy and more ridiculous.

Ginger Jane was always watching my every move. She cracked up when I made my first entrance onto the main stage in my enormous bunny ears. It was already a joke between us, since we had been comparing ear size in the dressing room. I spotted Ginger Jane giggling at me, and I laughed out loud as we exchanged looks. I responded by tossing the ears onto the floor behind me. Exiting the stage, I would put the ears back on to maintain the integrity of my costume.

It was still early, but the bar was filling up with people, as it was Friday afternoon. We usually got a huge rush-hour crowd that enjoyed happy hour until the traffic on the highways lightened up. As soon as I came onto the floor after my main stage dance, Ginger Jane grabbed my hand and said, "C'mon, Persia. My pilot friends are in town, and they want us to dance together for them in one booth."

The "friction," or lap dance, booths at the remodeled Stinkfinger Club were four-foot cubicles with glass block walls. Inside each booth were two round-back, lavender-colored chairs and a small table to set cocktails on. Ginger Jane just loved men of a darker persuasion and definitely preferred them over the fair-skinned male. Both of these men were islanders from Jamaica and successful commercial airline pilots. As we waited for a new song to play so we could give them the full benefit of a dance, I was fumbling around with my antennae like ears once more. Ginger Jane and I were cackling with laughter! I removed them and put them on my dance recipient. His skin was flawlessly smooth and black as night. He wore a white collared business shirt with a thin black necktie. The contrast of the white shirt against his skin and the black lights glowing in the booth made his skin even darker. He was very handsome and had a grin on his face like he was getting away with something. Men always seem to be such sports; but I am sure that he had a growing erection and could have cared less what my girlfriend and I were preoccupied with. He looked so silly and vulnerable with my bunny ears on, l I just couldn't resist the moment to be sarcastic. I looked at Ginger Jane and said, "You know, this definitely gives new meaning to the term 'jungle bunny.'" We laughed even louder at my joke and began our dance. It was an excellent evening with our pilot friends.

Fourteen

MONSTER-TRUCK COCK

One of the perks of being a stripper was working bachelor parties on the side. As you learned in earlier chapters, I have acquired near perfect skills from my predecessor, Cocaine Jane. Ginger Jane, my latest running mate, was raised on a farm and wanted a life of sophistication and elegance. She loved men and dancing as much as I did, but she hated the stigma and labels associated with being a stripper. Call me a whore all you want; I have no shame in what I do. I really believe that as long as two consenting adults have an agreement about sexual fun, then what business is it of anyone else?

Ginger Jane, on the other hand, was consumed with guilt. When we did parties, she liked to call herself a "party girl." I don't care if you call me a slut or whore; however, I do cringe with the word "prostitute," simply because I don't like the word. It is no fun at all! Call me what you want. Inside I felt strong, confident, and beautiful; like a princess. Ginger Jane sold herself cheaply to the point of sabotaging my business. I was constantly reminding her that we were not party girls looking for a free meal; we required roses, and lots of them, when we were wined and dined. The common phrase, "You can take the girl out of the country, but you can't take the country out of the girl" was Ginger Jane in a nutshell.

One of my regular Johns at this moment in time was a bail bonds-man. He was head-turning handsome, a blond Cuban with olive skin and green eyes. He had a stocky build, straight nose, square jaw, and a dazzling smile that might blind you if the sun was shining on his face. He usually had a three-day beard, and he wore black leather and a skull cap because he drove his Harley Davidson to the club often. Most men look stupid in this kind of costume, but not John. It was authentic on him, and he wore it naturally. He had a certain sarcasm and mischievousness that matched my own. He attempted to snag me as a girlfriend a couple of times, but intuitively, I knew he needed more than one woman to satisfy him, and that increased his sleaze factor to get his foot in the door with me.

One day, John approached me about working a bachelor party, a smaller one for his elite clientele. These men were judges and politi-cians, so the party was hush-hush, supersmall, and private. Instead of taking the usual five to six girls, I invited my new comrade, the tall redhead, Ginger Jane.

We arrived around seven in the evening at the downtown hotel in Miami. John met us on the top floor of the hotel at the elevators and escorted us to a presidential suite at the end of the hallway. The room was dark and full of men seated up against the wall so that we couldn't really see them. John had instructed us to perform a girl-girl show on the bed, which was dimly lit with lights shining on us. The atmosphere was a bit tense and not the usual animal house party scene that charac-terizes most bachelor parties,

John stopped us after about ten minutes and escorted us down the hall to another room. It seemed abrupt, and I thought maybe the men didn't like our show. John said, "Most of these guys want private time with you girls, so I am going to send them in one at a time and will settle up with you at the end of the night."

Ginger Jane and I were a great double team. I was more sultry and ready to please and Joni (Ginger Jane's real name) was all show and ready to tease. I loved sucking cock. Joni hated it. I swallowed; she didn't. She licked, slurped, and juggled balls, giggling the entire time. I would rather suck than fuck, but Ginger Jane preferred to fuck; in fact, she loved it. She had a deep pussy and had had a hysterectomy in her early thirties, so she had no equipment in the way to cause her pain like lots of women. Ginger Jane loved a good pounding during intercourse and enthusiastically expressed her pleasure during the act.

Choo choo! Whoa whoa! Here came the train! We must have serviced about ten guys when this six-foot-seven long-haired blond German piece of ass came sauntering in the room. He was wearing a gray Italian suit. Fuck! He was sooooo fine! He had huge feet, like a size sixteen, and when he pulled out his dong, we both stared at each other and gasped. Knowing how much Ginger Jane loved big cocks, I said, "Jane honey, he is all yours." I lay back on the bed and gladly watched this Fabio lookalike nail my friend. After he left, we couldn't stop talking about the size of his cock and his blue-ribbon performance.

John came in directly afterward, and we all started reviewing the evening. He laid all the roses on the bed for us. Ginger Jane snorted, "Wait a minute, you forgot about John, the guy with the long blond hair."

"Who?" questioned John with a puzzled look on his face.

"The guy with the monster-truck cock," I said, laughing.

"The big German guy wearing the gray suit with the long hair! He had a giant dick."

"There was no guy like that in our party!" John said with eyes gleaming. Ginger Jane was fuming and stomping about, complaining about the shortage of roses. John and I just figured out that this guy must have had a room on this floor and heard our moans and groans, wandered into our room, got lucky grabbing a free piece of ass, and left. We started laughing uncontrollably. Joni didn't find getting hosed down by monster-truck cock very funny at all! I would love to meet up with that hunk of a man one more time in my life just to pat him on the back and thank him for one of the funniest memories of my life.

Fifteen

THE BIG CHICKEN

Another day in the club: a large, wide-bodied man approached me. He had a round, handsome baby face. I noticed his hands; they were padded like a grizzly bear's. Fat John requested dances, and we immediately proceeded to a private booth.

"Persia, I would like you to go on a white-water rafting trip with me."

"I don't even know you! What makes you think I would go out with a stranger or even consider a trip with you?"

"I'm going to return in three weeks, and we will make plans then," Fat John said in a confident voice.

This John was a man of his word. He showed up exactly three weeks to the day. I was pleasantly surprised.

"Hello, beautiful! Are you ready to go white-water rafting?"

"I will go under one condition," I said firmly. "That I can take friends along with me."

I had two stripper friends in mind: my tall, crazy, redheaded girlfriend Ginger Jane and my favorite French stripper from Royal Gold. I called her my little French beignet. She was a svelte brunette with long, straight hair. She was sweet, uninhibited, and like a savvy panther on the prowl when it came to men. French Jane was a little on the thin side but had strong bones; her body was intoxicating and addicting. I used to love to go shopping with her. She would walk stark naked out of a dressing room to exchange clothes or ask my opinion and just turn heads and floor everybody in the place.

French Jane loved sex as much as I did. She loved to fuck; once she was fucking her partner, and in the midst of passion, they fell through the crack of the two twin beds pushed together and continued to fuck on the floor for an hour or more.

Ginger Jane had a wild side of her own. She preferred to be with young black athletes and wasted no time getting to know as many as she could, as fast as she could. It always amazed me when she was hurt and surprised after another fling did a hit-and-run on her pussy again. She stood five-toot-ten and had big, round, alluring blue eyes like a cartoon cat and short hair, deep red in color. Her hair and blue eyes were perfectly contrasted to her peach-colored skin. Her body was athletic and strong, and she had a beautiful, clear smile that was almost pirate like when she laughed hard.

Ginger Jane and I got to know each other quickly in the dressing room. Privacy was the best policy if one chose to work in a strip club, but since I was wild and uninhibited, that defeated that idea. Ginger Jane and I became famous friends fast! I was an easy mark to her generous compliments.

She loved my dark, smooth skin and loved big breasts to the point of obsession. Before our shift would start, we would give each other lap dances, and Ginger Jane would have her face buried in my big breasts while lightly scratching the front center of my thong with her long, perfect french nails.

Since I was going to have a partner on the excursion, I wanted my girl-friends to also have chaperones. Ginger Jane had a man in mind already. He resided in Atlanta, so the plan was to meet him once we arrived.

Now, I had an ex-boyfriend who was a perfect match for French Jane; he was on a desperate mission to marry a stripper, and the French girl was just his type. Remember the guy with the fake ring? That one! He also bought fast cars (pussy wagons) to attract women. At the time, he had a black 911 Porsche.

He was smitten with her the moment they met. Porsche John insisted that I go shopping with him to buy her some diamond earrings. "Should I buy her zirconia or the real thing?" he asked me, and I said, "Go for the real ones; she is worth it."

I guess it wasn't the best advice, since she lost one on the first date.

So our trip was set. Fat John started booking the flights and lodging. We were to be away three days and navigate the Ocoee and Chattooga rivers in Georgia. We were flying on ValuJet Airlines. Remember them? None of our seats were together, and worse than that, it was mid-July, and the air conditioner wasn't working on the plane. Porsche John walked up to my seat, and with a very flat expression, asked me if I had a blanket he could use. We both busted out laughing, since the plane felt like it was 120 degrees!

When we arrived in Atlanta, we loaded up a rented Lincoln town car and were off to meet Ginger Jane's latest conquest at a brewery bar downtown. What a surprise! Her beau didn't show up. That was predictable and par for the course. We got past that wrinkle and decided to kick the trip off the right way and went to the Taj Mahal strip club to look at some pussy. Fat John had deep pockets, and three strippers in a club as patrons was a dangerous combo. French Jane was laughing and getting as many dances as Fat John would buy her. Fat John was a real party animal and appeared to want everyone to have a good time. He was heavyset and not my type, but we were all having a blast already with a nice blend of personalities. Porsche John was acting like the fourth girl in the group.

He liked Fat John taking over and didn't so much as give a head fake when the bill came. Loser! He had become like a brother to me, and I was annoyed with him as if he were my sibling. He had been with

French Jane for five hours now and had his head so far up her ass that he could hardly speak or look at anything else.

We had about six girls dancing around us now. The structure of the club seemed to go on forever. It had multiple levels with gorgeous dancers on each tier. The walls were lined with heavy satin red-and-purple drapes. It was the most luxurious club I had ever been in. After two hours, it was time to get on the road to our first cabin.

I'm uncomfortably shy when I first start hanging out with someone. I had made it clear to Fat John that just because he offered to take me on a trip, that it wasn't permission for a piece of my ass. He respected my wishes, but I knew this was going to be a four-day battle.

We arrived at our cabin around nine that evening. I drew in a deep breath, smelling the oak trees and woodsy scents of the mid-South I so missed while living in Florida. The guys started unloading our luggage from the trunk of the town car. Uh-oh! Where was my suitcase? You would think one of these guys would have picked up my bag while I took my seat in the car. I was screaming inside! No makeup, no clothing, no deodorant, no goddamn contact solution!

The cabin was spacious and quite nice. Porsche John nabbed the master bedroom for Frenchie and himself. I cornered him face to face with teeth gritted and snarling, "What makes you think you get first choice of bedrooms?"

"I walked in first, and besides, I want to fuck Frenchie!" he teased.

"Fat John organized this trip, and we should have the master bedroom!" I reasoned.

Porsche John dug his heels in and shut the door in my face with my nose fighting the crack to the last push.

Aarrrrgggghhhhh! The situation was getting worse. Big John and I had to take the smaller bedroom with a queen-size bed, and the Ginger Jane got the sofa bed in the living room.

First things first: I needed to locate my luggage. I called Budget Rent a Car.

"Sir, my group just rented the town car from you, and we left my luggage at the curb."

"Yes, ma'am. We have your luggage. Can you tell me where you are located?"

"Yeah, sure. We are in the woods in Georgia in a cabin!" I exclaimed jokingly.

I asked Fat John the address, and they both laughed at me. We were so far off the beaten path, we probably were in Bumfuck, Egypt—that imaginary place all southern rednecks use to describe someplace not on the map. Unable to give this man directions, he very kindly came up with a solution. In a very slow southern drawl, he said, "Ma'am, I know this may sound crazy, but have you ever heard of the Big Chicken?"

"What? The Big Chicken?" I asked.

Then I asked the group if they had heard of the Big Chicken. More laughter and a unanimous chorus of no.

"Well, ma'am, it is a famous landmark in Georgia. Meet me tomorrow at one o'clock at the Big Chicken in Marietta, and I will bring your luggage. You can ask anyone where it is.

"Okay, thank you. See you there. Good-night."

Great! This Fat John gets to see the real me, au naturel. I was so uncomfortable at that moment. Ginger Jane shared her toothbrush with me, and we created a makeshift case for my contact lens. It was getting late, and the lovebirds were tucked away, so we decided to go to sleep. I curled up in the bed on my left side facing the window with all my clothes on, practically holding my breath. I was begging in my head, "Please don't let him touch me!"

The cabin was so quiet you could hear a pin drop. All of a sudden, the house sounded like it had a large bumblebee inside. Oh God! Don't tell me Ginger Jane was masturbating with her vibrator! Fat John and I started giggling hysterically. I thought I would die of embarrassment at that moment. "Jane, what are you doing out there?" I yelled.

Exhausted and overwhelmed, I managed to fall asleep.

We all got up in the morning and had breakfast, loaded up the car, and were ready to head for the river. Frenchie was taking a very long shower. Thirty minutes later we were all banging on the door. What was taking her so long? Finally, Ginger Jane and I made our way into the bathroom to find Frenchie spread-eagle with the water full blast, beating down on her clitoris.

Frenchie was a playful little devil. The three of us started giggling, and Ginger Jane and I started playing with her. Porsche John was listening outside the door, getting jealous.

"Let me in!" he demanded.

We finally dug her out of the tub with a major group effort and piled in the car. The ride to the Ocoee was about thirty minutes. Fat John was the only one in our group who had been white-water rafting. The rest of us were excited and somewhat anxious. We took the crash course in navigating the river, and that was intimidating. Our raft guide's name was Noah. That was appropriate, since we were all a bunch of animals.

It was a hot summer day, and it gave us three strippers good reason to shed our shirts and wear our life jackets over our bras. This was scary and thrilling. Fat John anchored the right front side of the raft with me to his side. Porsche John was opposite him with Frenchie at his side looking like a frail bird. Ginger Jane was perched on the back of the raft with Noah at the helm. All I could think about was foot entrapment and the end of my dancing career. What if I fell in the river and got my foot trapped under a rock.

All of a sudden, bumpety-bump, and I was overboard and swimming. Frenchie's facial expression made it worse; you would have thought I was drowning. I wasn't sure that I wasn't!

I started screaming, "Get my oar! Get my oar!"

Everyone but Frenchie was laughing hysterically at me. My arms felt about six inches long as I swirled around and kept trying to elevate my feet out of the water. It seemed like an eternity before Noah grabbed the back of my life vest and threw me into the boat. Once safely in the raft, I felt refreshed and invigorated! Frenchie and Porsche John were spooked after my swim and jumped at every rapid.

Four hours later we were eating a home-cooked feast at Pat's Place, then off to the Big Chicken. Well, the man at Budget was right: the Big Chicken was not hard to find. Located at a KFC was a twenty-foot metal chicken with one cockeyed, swirling eyeball. We all had a good laugh at the famous landmark, and I was relieved to have a change of clothes and my toothbrush.

Our group was off to the more difficult Chattooga River. By now, Porsche John had decided that Frenchie was going to be his wife. They had had enough of white-water rafting already and opted to spend the next day in the cabin and screw rather than wrestle another river.

It was Ginger Jane, Fat John, and me. Our next cabin was a quaint A-frame cottage. Naturally, Porsche John hustled into the master suite, and Fat John and I got a cozy loft bedroom. Ginger Jane was back on the couch.

Fat John and I had bonded and decided to have a few beers on the back porch. For a moment alone in the kitchen, John put his arms around my waist and started to kiss me, when Ginger Jane came walking in to sabotage our romantic interlude. Fat John muttered under his breath, "Fuck me!" Ginger Jane was flitting around the room, teasing us, when Frenchie heard the commotion and wanted to be a part of the fun. Porsche John was trying to corral his bride back into the bedroom, but she was already bored with his smothering ways. Ginger Jane, Fat John, Frenchie, and I ended up in the bathroom with the faucet going full blast. I pulled Fat John in by the shirt, and we locked the other John out.

I gave Frenchie a french kiss and pulled Fat John in close to join us. I was blowing his mind! They were both sexy kissers with soft, pink lips and very clean mouths. I thought Fat John would come in his pants, but Porsche John's impatience interrupted all our fun. He managed to convince Frenchie to go back to the bedroom, but once he fell asleep, she was drinking beer with us on the porch. Everyone finally went to sleep, but Big John and I decided to stay up the rest of the night. Around 2:00 a.m. I got sleepy and decided to lie down for a while. Fat John followed me in. We lay down together; finally, he could make his move now. His lips just barely touched mine when Ginger Jane screamed up to our open loft bedroom. "What you guys doing up there?"

"Fuck me!" John complained again. This happened a few more times, as if Ginger Jane had a mirror and could see John's every attempt to kiss me. Fat John started laughing and said, "I don't even know that woman, but I love her!"

Within seconds she was upstairs orchestrating the sex between John and me. "Kiss her, John!"

Ginger Jane was a voyeur and loved to watch people fornicate. We were laughing but managed to maintain some carnal heat in the moment. Frenchie escaped once more and desperately wanted to be with us, but Porsche John snatched her back to the bedroom.

I was naked by now with Big John fucking me like a stallion. He flipped me over and mounted me doggie style. Ginger Jane started slapping my ass and then propped my tennis shoes on my feet. We all lost it laughing. She had this lilting laugh that was contagious. Finally, they were both on top of me, taking turns fingering and fucking me until I squirted all over them, the bed, and everywhere. Ginger Jane and I passed out, arms wrapped around each other with Big John resorting to the couch.

One hour of sleep passed all too fast. Hungover and sleep deprived, we drove to the staging area of the river. Holy shit! We had to carry the raft on our heads for about a half mile before starting a five-hour raft ride. We were paired with a lesbian couple, one of whom acted like she had written the book on white-water rafting. The Chattooga River was more severe than the Acoe. It also happened to be the location river for the movie *Deliverance*. The dominant female took charge of the front of the raft, much to Big John's chagrin. Our guide lectured us for a few minutes before we tackled each rapid. The seriousness of this river put the fear of God in us. Ginger Jane and I screamed our lungs out, paddling furiously through each rapid. Big John was in his glory, beating his head against the waves as if to challenge the river itself. During a calm interlude, the butch lady started a conversation about snakes.

"There was a snake in our bedroom last night!" Ginger Jane chirped. Fat John got the joke and beamed a big smile, unable to contain a profuse laugh. "Oh God!" he muttered like he was thinking "Here she goes again."

"Oh yeah? What kind of snake was it?" the bull dyke asked.

"It was really big and kind of beige colored," she devilishly laughed with her big blue eyes dancing.

I was embarrassed all over again, but was amused at the mutual lack of concern Fat John and Ginger Jane had for social acceptance. Our lesbo captain never caught on, and we laughed uncontrollably. The memory of our antics from a few hours earlier was fresh in our mind, and we were enjoying our perverted secret among us without including our rafting comrades.

The river, the picnic, and the day were exhilarating. Sadly enough, our adventure had come to an end. You can bet that whenever anyone in our group passes a KFC, all the great memories of the Big Chicken trip will come rushing back. As for Frenchie and Porsche John, he bought her a Rolex watch, and she disappeared, never to be heard from again. Ginger Jane is living happily ever after with an older white man. Porsche John and I remain friends and continue to confide and advise through our romances. Fat John gets another chapter in the book.

Sixteen

FOOT FETISH

Foot fetishes I presume aren't something the general public thinks about, unless of course you have a foot fetish or you are in my shoes. I never was really focused on feet. My mother was always commenting on how beautiful my hands and feet were and that the first thing she noticed when I was born were my long fingers and my long eyelashes.

Gentlemen's clubs are the perfect playground to express unusual fantasies. Foot men of this sort are common in the clubs. Most of the time they are men with shallow pockets who hang around waiting for the weary dancer with tired feet so that they can have a chance to indulge her in a foot massage.

All the dancers participated in this luxury once we had made a few bucks and had throbbing feet from wearing pointed stilettos (platforms only became fashionable again in the late nineties).

One spring day in 1995, a tall man with a stocky build walked into the bar. He had a short, red buzz haircut and a pasty white complexion. He wore a square-cut, brown leather jacket with big patch like pockets stitched to the front; below, he wore blue jeans and yellow-suede construction boots.

I nabbed him quickly and ushered him to a booth for a private dance. There were five booths facing the bar, and John and I entered the last one on the south end. This booth was still in clear view of the bar. As I was doing my dance, sliding and slithering on John, he made a request.

He really liked the stockings I was wearing and wanted to buy them. As much as I hated to part with my costume accessories, I agreed to sell them for thirty dollars. I continued to dance for John for several dances. On about the fourth dance, John asked if I would slip his left boot off. I was already in an upside-down position on his lap with my head near his feet. His request amused me, and I wanted to share my amusement with my coworker.

I whispered loudly and urgently to Brad the bartender, "Psssttt! Brad! Check this out!" Steve had worked at this bar since the seventies and had seen pretty much everything. As Brad watched from the corner of the bar, I removed John's boot to expose a thick foot and an ankle donned in a black, sheer stocking. Maybe Brad hadn't seen it all; his eyes bugged out of his head, and his O-shaped mouth mirrored my own. We both had to squelch an irresistible urge to laugh. I continued to entertain Brad by pulling up John's jeans and exposing the pantyhose-lined calf. How odd to see a big, masculine man like John in female stockings rather than the usual white athletic sock one would expect in a construction boot. This was outrageous and so funny to me! John continued with more requests. I tore off his stocking around his toes and began to fondle and play with his foot.

I could almost hear Brad the bartender gasp at that moment and felt his retreat to the other end of the bar.

Not long after pantyhose John, I encountered another customer in the same bar. I consented to give the gentleman a lap dance and when we entered the booth, the man asked "Persia, can I just rub your feet?" I just love these foot guys—so sensual, soothing, and sexy to have my feet worshiped, kissed, and played with and get paid for it at the same time. I find it quite complimentary for a man to choose my feet over my lips, breasts, ass, and genitals. "Sure!" I told John, "Would you like my toes in your mouth?" After our dances, John begged me not to mention his foot fetish to the friends he was there with. It was personal to him. His group was at the bar today celebrating his bachelor party. The best part of his story was he confessed that his bride-to-be also had a foot fetish! Now, that was a marriage made in heaven.

I really love dancing on the main stage. It was the place I could let it all hang out and dance to the songs that I chose. I have always had an insatiable appetite for attention and was in all my glory as a true exhibitionist. One day a lanky man with curly brown hair and wire-rimmed glasses came up to the edge of the main stage while I was dancing. I smiled and leaned down to greet him. "I love the coral-colored polish on your toenails," he said. Oh yes! I thought. A foot nerd!

When we ended up in a booth, he had a slightly different approach. John commented that he noticed that I had a knack for acting and had a special proposition for me, but did not want to discuss it in the club and wanted to meet me on the outside. He promptly called me a couple of days later and wanted to meet me at a hotel. He had a request for coral or red toenails, of course, which I had learned were two preferred colors for the foot fetish guys. John also requested that I wear a tight black dress, black stockings, no panties, very dark, black sunglasses and red full lips plus have a bitchy, dominating attitude.

My kind of guy—I liked this role. I arrived at his Motel 6 hotel room, and he very carefully let me in. John immediately got on all fours and started reaching up my dress and rubbing my thighs. Are you ready for this? No you are not...the weirdo started to bark on my pussy. "Ruff, ruff, woof, woof."

Okay, I said to myself, be a bitch; do not laugh in his face. I was amazed: the vibration and ridiculous act of barking was getting me very wet and turned me on almost to the brink of orgasm. Jesus! John then slipped off my high heels and asked me to walk around on my tiptoes. He slowly started to rip the toes out of my stockings and had me continue to tiptoe across the room. John remained on his hands and knees the entire time. What came next was a total surprise. Ready? No, you are not!

He pulled out his dick, slapped it on the floor, and requested that I smash it with my long, painted toes. My brain screamed at me, "Don't laugh; be a bitch!" I kept a straight face and began to smash his limp member between my toes until he grabbed it up and jerked it off with splendor. I had filled his request.

Now for his proposition. John and his partner were quite good at beating casino games and hired actress types as their mules. The pay was good, but the potential consequences weren't worth the risk. I would rather just smash his cock and have him bark on me—that was a relatively harmless game.

My next adventure had me laughing out loud for months. I had been published in several magazines by now, and the Internet was still a non-fertile place for networking. I received lots of snail mail from my fans for my publications in *Gent Magazine* (August 1999), *Cheri* (1999 and 2000), and *Gallery* and *Score* (1999). Most of the mail came from lonely prisoners desperate for human contact and someone to pen pal with and con out of money.

One unusual letter came from a handsome probation officer from Nebraska. He sent photos and loving cards and was so nice that one day I decided to call him. John was really stunned by my phone call and expressed his desire to praise and worship me. After several weeks of correspondence, I agreed to give him fifteen minutes of prepaid phone sex. One night John called me and nervously said that he had a special request. Are you ready? No, you are not! Nebraska John said he would be forever indebted to me if he could purchase my clipped, french-painted toenails in an envelope. I expressed how flattered I was and made a deal to sell them for fifty dollars. Thank fuck it was a phone transaction and not a face-to-face request.

I hung up the phone and laughed uncontrollably. Wanting to share the moment with someone, I called a favorite relative who shared my sense of humor, and we laughed together about it time after time. Some things in life give you gray hair and others give you joy. Selling my clipped toenails definitely gave me joy!

CONCUPISCENT ECSTASY

Oh, how the aroma of her sweet beauteous pussy

as she titillates herself, her heat, strike me with ecstasy.

Her soft moans, her fingers rubbing unto her wet

clitoris–

temptation ushers me in, heightens my lust with bliss.

My soft, succulent lips began to journey amongst her

thighs.

Seventeen

CANDY-CANE JANE

When I think of the song "Sex and Candy," my girl Candy-Cane Jane comes to my mind. Tall, blond, blue eyed, and built for sex, Candy-Cane Jane had strong legs, a perfect ass, and a face like an angel. She was a Brooklyn blend of Irish and Puerto Rican. The first time I saw her, she was speaking Spanish to another dancer in the dressing room at the Stinkfinger Club. I had never seen a blonde beauty speaking fluent Spanish. Candy-Cane Jane intimidated me, and I didn't make friends with strippers anyhoo!

At some point, Candy-Cane Jane must have been observing me bouncing around the club making money that eventually motivated her to latch on to me. Our contact inside the club was minimal, since I worked mostly on the day shift and Candy-Cane Jane worked late shift. When our shifts overlapped, Candy-Cane Jane would stay close to me. At Stinkfinger, I had several regulars. One John in particular was a flamboyant, crazy guy who liked to have an entourage of girls in the champagne room every time he came to the club. He had severe arthritis, and his usual routine was to get a fast buzz on tequila shots and then take off his shoes and pants, leaving only his shirt, his Calvin Klein underwear, and his fanny pack full of cash and sex toys. I kept my distance as he appeared to like younger women, and honestly, he intimidated me as my new blond girlfriend did.

John was tall and slender with a sexy, baritone voice and wore a big straw hat. Never in my wildest dreams could I have conjured up the stories I lived with these two wonderful people. I became John's go-to girl. He would get me high on tequila, champagne, and pussy. After an hour of getting a good buzz on, John would order food from the Hooter's next door and insist that I bring another girl to our party.

Candy-Cane Jane couldn't wait to be invited up. It was the early days of the champagne room, which means that it went almost unnoticed. Very few entertainers went to the champagne room, and a dancer could hang there for an entire shift, and as long as the champagne was flowing, management didn't care.

Once the girls started noticing my frequency in the champagne room, the jealousy started, and everything changed. Champagne prices went up, and bouncers started peeking in every five minutes. On top of that, for every stage rotation that a dancer missed, she would have to pay the DJ ten dollars. All of these things happened four years down the road. For now, we were busy inventing the champagne room and making history at Goldfinger.

John and I got my new girlfriend dancing immediately for us. In all our enthusiasm and with nobody paying any attention to us, I had Candy-Cane Jane upside down on my lap with her G-string off and my face deep in her fleshy, pink pussy. Candy-Cane Jane giggled as I played with her.

"Jane, your pussy is the best ham sandwich I have ever tasted." That statement bound us together like glue. Our time together at first was brief most of the time, since we had only an hour of overlapping shifts to work together. The fact was that I had a new friend, and things were going to ignite between two hot women with burning fuses about to be lit by a flame.

In the nineties, bachelor parties were a popular trend. I started getting calls to organize parties. Men preferred as many girls as possible at these events, but without a doubt I needed at least one other girl. I had developed trust in Candy-Cane Jane enough, to call her for one of these parties.

She jumped at the chance, and I drove over to pick her up at her townhouse near the club, and then off we went to the Marriott at Beach Place in Ft. Lauderdale. I always anticipated problems when interacting with stripper girls. But I thought Jane was cheerful, bright eyed, sober, and had a ready-and-willing attitude. The party was typical and uneventful. It is always a bonus if the men are respectful, not jeering and creepy or making degrading, crass remarks. So many men stereotype strippers and file them into a sleazy category, assuming that since women undress for money, that gives men a green light to verbally abuse them. Fortunately, none of those types were at this party.

Everyone was laughing and letting the good times roll! Bachelor parties are events that you want to get in and out of, not linger. Leave the hungry wolves wanting more. I was watching the clock and finished our act and entertainment fashionably within two hours. It was time to go home after a fun night's work.

Outside the hotel, Candy-Cane Jane and I started walking down the beach front, the neon lights from local establishments flickering all around us. How I love the neon lights! Candy-Cane Jane gently grabbed my arm and stopped walking. "Where are we going now, Persia?"

"Home!" I said.

"All you ever do is work! You never want to go out!" Candy-Cane Jane complained.

I replied, "Well, look at us. The two of us together will cause a riot in a public place!" I exclaimed.

Jane and I both had long legs. She was wearing a black miniskirt and a tight V-neck sleeveless top and black patent leather stilettos. I was wearing a long-sleeved, scoop-neck cocoa-brown T-shirt with matching suede miniskirt and six-inch brown suede Charles Jourdan pumps. Both outfits were alluring and provocative.

Jane continued to plead, and I finally consented, feeling guilty for being such a buzzkill. Right in the beach place complex there was a two-story, gargantuan nightclub called Atlantis. We decided that would be a fun club to follow up our bachelor party with.

When we entered the club, I felt like I had walked onto a movie set. Heads turned in our direction, jaws dropped, and the crowd of people literally parted to let us walk by as they stared at us. In an instant, we were escorted to the first bar with sixteen shots of tequila waiting that a patron had already purchased for us. We both slammed a couple of shots and started dancing with each other. Others started dancing alongside us, but people around us were mostly watching. Wherever I went, I was onstage. The club seemed to have an endless ceiling.

Atlantis could hold at least a thousand people. There was a live band on an elevated stage, about five satellite bars with three main ones in the club. The outside patio was huge and had a gazebo and yet another bar. Atlantis was rocking, and the alcohol was pouring like a river. Oh yes, these were my tequila and margarita days.

When I get loose, I want to get naked and get everybody else naked with me! I am an unmerciful tease. I kept Candy-Cane Jane in a passionate lip lock most of the time, and we both took turns pulling each other's skirts and tops up, revealing our thongs and bras. The panty set I was wearing was an eye opener, as it was chocolate brown like my outerwear with a shiny, pale-yellow, woven, embroidered flower pattern. Candy-Cane Jane was always the quintessential slut. It was genetic…the Puerto Rican in her for sure.

Girls were coming up to me telling me how much they loved my girlfriend. Jane was so amazingly striking with natural blond hair, golden tan skin, and blue eyes, and she towered over six feet tall in her heels. Her lips were pouty and luscious.

I knew she really lusted for me, because with every kiss, her pupils would dilate and change color from light blue to black. It was an erotic sight to behold. Her presence would draw me in with those eyes staring at me while she softly caressed my mouth. She was married, and her husband was dark complected as I was, so I know she was attracted to dark skin, hair, and eyes.

With our sexual display of kissing and flashing, the crowd was getting restless with all the sexual tension we created. I wasn't so sure that my statement about causing a riot might just become a reality. Quite intoxicated, we decided before all hell broke loose to get out of Atlantis. We left arm in arm and stumbled to my car, giggling and very proud of our performance.

The Mayfair

"Those were the days, my *friend*. We thought they'd never end. We'd sing and dance forever and a day. We'd fight and never lose—those were the days, oh yes, those were the days, la la la la la la la…"

That old song from 1968 comes to mind when I think of all the good times with my Candy-Cane Jane.

In the seventies and eighties, I had friends that I partied with at discotheques; we stacked our twenty-five-cent empty beer cups to the ceiling while dancing on a lit dance floor and whirling around doing the bump and the hustle while a silver globe above our heads was flashing images on our faces and bodies.

With the nineties came rave clubs and ecstasy. It was still legal, and young adults would roll in groups at clubs and be mesmerized by alternative, mind-expanding music. Disco balls were replaced by guys with neon glowing ropes in hand, dancing with snakelike movements in the dark, enhancing the psychedelic roll the crowd was experiencing.

One of the waitresses I knew at Stinkfinger had an endless supply of ecstasy and was always walking around with a shit-eating grin on her face. One day I gave in and bought some from her; these were the days of maniacs and strawberries (names for ex pills).

Candy Cane Jane loved to do ecstasy, and she loved me when I was on it too. I would become even more sexual when I was high on ecstasy—if that was possible. I became a possessed, writhing, sensual, climactic sex organ! I could orgasm with a light wind blowing around my body on that stuff!

One New Year's Eve, we ended up at the Theater, a new name for one of those gargantuan clubs in Fort Lauderdale that never made it financially. They just changed the decor, name, and owners. We entered the place after eating a roll, and I remember it was all lit in green. Rave clubs didn't have that bouncy dance energy; instead, it was upbeat and very sexual, with everyone lounging on couches with a laid-back buzz.

As soon as we sat down, we screamed with glee! One of the waitresses from Stinkfinger was working here at the Theater. She had been fired from Stinkfinger a year earlier for skimming off liquor sales. I loved her style anyway. She hadn't changed a bit and brought us a couple of rounds of free margaritas to celebrate our reunion. Next, one of the old bouncers from Stinkfinger walked up, and it was like old times. He was all pumped up on steroids, complete with a high-pitched voice and a little head compared to his body.

I was having an excellent time with Joni 4 until my fat wannabe boyfriend showed up to scold us and spoil our good time. I guess it was a good thing he did show up, as we were in no shape to drive. I started looking around and all of a sudden, Joni 4 was gone. She had told me she was going to the restroom when Fat Boy showed up, but she rarely went without me, and she had been gone too long.

I started to search the room for her. Finally, we found her. She was upset and crying. Evidently, the numb nuts bouncer had forced himself on her and raped her in the men's room. He had always been so friendly to us. It was a lousy ending on New Year's Eve.

Candy Cane Jane and I always seemed to have disastrous endings to what started as a wonderful time. I was always the party organizer and played madam 99.9 percent of the time.

It was a pleasant surprise when Jane finally hooked us up one time.

We were going to get a huge donation from her new clients after our rendezvous at the beautiful Mayfair Hotel in Coconut Grove. Naturally, Candy-Cane Jane wanted to roll that day. The party was set for lunchtime for five or six high-profile Latin men. I was impressed when we met them. They were sophisticated, well-dressed men and had the champagne flowing with a big tray of fresh fruit.

Jane had not eaten that morning, and after her second glass of champagne, she had to run to the bathroom. One of the men ran after her to help. Oh, this was just great! I was so embarrassed. She started puking loudly, shit all over herself, then passed out semiconscious on the floor.

All the men panicked and quickly left the scene, as it appeared a 911 call might be in order. Candy-Cane Jane was very strong physically and mentally. I began slapping her while splashing her with cold water and threatening to call her husband if she didn't snap out of it. She was the rock in her dysfunctional family, in which she lived in the midst of incest, homosexuality, HIV, heroin addiction, and all kinds of trouble on both sides. As bad as she was, the thought of being weak or having to face her husband in a crisis situation woke her right up. I wiped her ass, pulled her up to stand, and got the hell out of there. So much for her leading us to a successful day.

Maybe Fat Boy was right. He always said she was just trouble and that I was pussy whipped.

New York

Guido and I traditionally traveled to New York City for our birthdays every year, his in March and mine in late September. In September 1997, we agreed to take Candy-Cane Jane, since she and Guido were both Brooklynites. It seemed like a fun and natural thing to do. As we always did, we stayed at the glorious Waldorf Astoria Hotel on Park Avenue, with a room in the Tower, Guido style. One thing about Guido, he went all out when it came to having a good time. We rode in limos the entire trip.

The first thing Candy Cane Jane did upon arrival was steal a spoon at the hotel and put it in her bag as a souvenir. Poor child hadn't been out of her Bay Ridge neighborhood much, obviously. I scolded her and attempted to teach her about how to behave properly and the difference between right and wrong.

Next, we were off to a new, hot club: Twila. Guido and his friend paid the cover charge, and Candy Cane Jane and I, being girls, were off to the powder room. All the stalls were occupied and in one of them, we got the drift that a girl was smoking a joint. Joni was impatient and ready to party. She didn't appreciate the girl taking up space for party favors, and being the Brooklyn chick that she was, she busted open the door, grabbed the girl by the shirt, and punched her in the nose when she talked back to her.

Uh-oh! I grabbed Candy-Cane Jane, Guido, and his friend and left before the real fight started. So far, we couldn't take this whore anywhere! We ended up barhopping until we ended up in some blue-collar dive in Joni's old neighborhood. I hated the place, but we all got a good buzz on and blondie and I passed out in our room and woke up and ate eighty-five-dollar pancakes for breakfast.

Even though Jane was a New Yorker, she hadn't seen any of the museums or sights in the city. Guido and I were ready to share some of our favorite places that had become rituals on our excursions while in Manhattan. Typically, Guido and I went to the World Trade Center at 11:00 a.m. for coffee, just before the lunch crowd arrived. Jane was in awe of the building. It was a sunny day and sunlight poured through the glass walls of the trade center.

Before taking the elevator up to the Windows on the World restaurant, Jane and I walked around the lobby, and she wanted to tour the building, so up the escalator we went. After a quick tour, Jane was ready to go to the top of the building and see the view that Guido and I had so often raved about. Jane and I were the only two people descending on the escalator to the main floor. Guido was waiting for us by the elevator. As Jane and I were going down, two Hindi women and their child were going up. They were a family: a grandmother, daughter, and granddaughter.

The grandmother was dressed in a traditional sari with sandals, while the mother and daughter wore western-style clothing. Jane and I witnessed the mother and daughter encouraging the frightened grandmother that the escalator was safe to ride. She was fragile and just terrified, but with her family's encouragement, she stepped on the up escalator then immediately panicked and fell. The young girl, who was around eleven years old, started screaming and crying, and the daughter was anxious and starting to come unglued.

Jane and I leapt over to the other side and grabbed the old woman under the arms. She was petite but dead weight in all her terror and started falling backward. I envisioned her garment getting sucked and tangled in the teeth of the escalator. Adrenaline and muscle took over, and Candy-Cane Jane and I heaved the old woman to safety and comforted the daughter and wiped the crocodile tears of the granddaughter.

It seems like only in New York do events like this happen daily. The first time I stepped onto a street in Manhattan, I saw the wheel come flying off a Cadillac and barrel down an avenue. Not one person who witnessed it missed a beat or seemed to care. I was astonished! That would have made the newspaper at that time in Memphis, my hometown.

Jane and I were glad to help the Indian family and couldn't wait to tell Guido our story. The elevators in the World Trade Center were massive inside and rose to the top of the building at lightning speed. As the doors opened, we were greeted by a beautiful, young black woman with an all-American smile. She had on a rainbow uniform to match the rainbow-carpeted wall behind her. Guido never missed a photo op. After all, that is what we came here for. Candy-Cane Jane, like everyone else who comes to Windows on the World for the first time, was impressed with this panoramic view of the city, the bridges, and the sight of Brooklyn and New Jersey from the top of the building. We all drank cappuccinos and then continued with our day shopping and eating like the queens of the city.

Three days of rolling and partying was plenty in the Big Apple. Yes, it was time for our trip to come to an end, but not before Guido had one more shrimp roll from Vincent's in Little Italy. We were flying out of Kennedy Airport at 1:00 p.m. Sad to leave, we piled in our stretch limousine.

The shrimp rolls at Vincent's Restaurant melted in your mouth. Guido had a mouthful, but his napkin was dripping with too much sauce. Now, I was forever busting his balls for littering. Everybody I have ever met from Brooklyn was a notorious litterbug—a pet peeve of mine!

What happened next seemed to happen in slow motion. The sunroof was open on this bright, sunny day in Little Italy. Guido was scarfing down his shrimp roll and had too much sauce on his napkin. He tossed it out of the open sun roof, and the napkin landed inside of a Chinese lady's car window. She got out of the car screaming and grabbed a rookie cop, who just happened to be Chinese.

He pulled the limo over and attempted to resolve the dispute. The entire time I was crying, "I told you so," and Candy-Cane Jane was ready to beat up the Chinese woman. She was crawling through the sunroof to get to her while I pulled on her legs, trying to keep her inside the vehicle. Somehow, we conned our way out of the ticket and miraculously made it to Kennedy to catch our flight. Guido wasn't too fond of my girlfriend after this trip, but I continued to hang out with her for more adventures ahead.

Lost Money

Party! Party! Party! Lot of ecstasy and lots of vodka. That was our medicine when we were on our playground. Fat Boy wannabe boyfriend used to wait up for me like a parent monitoring my every move, concerned that Candy-Cane Jane was big trouble and going to bring me down. Killjoy!

Jane and I had a terrific time in the midst of our substance abuse. I had a white 328 BMW that we would travel in. I had a party organized one night with some high-profile African American guys. Important people brought out the groupie side of Candy-Cane Jane, who most of the time was underwhelmed by anybody. She even brought a new stripper girlfriend from the club to assist us with entertaining. Jane also informed me that this girl had the smallest pussy I would ever see. I love freaks and couldn't wait to see it!

The party started when we arrived, and I took care of business first as always. The ex we popped that night was fresh and extremely good. I was just starting to peak when we were playing with this luscious Italian girl's very small twat. It was freaky! Much too tiny for my taste.

Candy-Cane Jane suddenly went into the bathroom and wanted me in there with her. She had a habit at the club and elsewhere of obsessively counting her money over and over.

"Persia! Our money is gone! I went to my purse to count the money you gave me, and it is gone!"

"What?" I yelled. "Where did you put it?"

Candy-Cane Jane started accusing the guys of sneaking in the bedroom and possibly going through our purses. I was immediately annoyed and embarrassed for her. I reluctantly went to the host of the party, and he and I were in total agreement that our Puerto Rican friend had made a mistake. The situation really had my feathers ruffled, and unlike with an alcohol buzz, where I would get sober from getting angry, my senses became even more heightened. I was pissed off and not even sure who to be mad at. The host said he would take care of me anyway, but he was baffled and angry too.

We all decided to go clubbing in Boca Raton and had a great time, but all I could think about was our lost money. My frustration level was so high that it ruined my night, and we went home. Candy-Cane Jane and Miss Tiny Twat were off to Brooklyn the next morning.

It was hockey mom time at my house and time to take the boys to the game.

Next, I did an odd thing. Before gathering up the boys, I went out to the garage and walked over to the passenger side of the car and opened the back door. Why? It must have been an angel on my shoulder. On the floor I found $1,600 and eight condoms in a pile. That dumb slut Jane had put the money in her purse, and it had fallen out in her search for ecstasy. The greedy girl always had to have her claws on the money.

Being the honest or stupid person (whatever your viewpoint may be), I called her immediately to tell her I had found her money. Guido would have told me to not tell her and keep the money for my trouble, but that action never crossed my mind. My relief was not in finding the money but the fact that the children didn't find it first!

Christmas Party

Candy-Cane Jane was about ten years younger than I was. You would think she would have lots more energy than I did, but to my surprise, she had a hard time keeping up. It was Christmastime and full season in Florida. This was the time when all the establishments, including strippers, made their dough.

"Are you ready for a good day?" I asked Jane. "We have parties starting at eleven this morning until three the next morning. Time to bank!" I cheered.

I had instructed Candy-Cane Jane to bring a Christmas outfit, stockings, G-strings, baby wipes, toys, and condoms. Our first stop was a warehouse for a lawn mower service. We were lap dancing on Toro mowers. Jane was apprehensive and thought I was a nut job, but the parties got better as the day went along. We made a bundle of cash, and I had a big smile on my face. Merry Christmas to me!

As usual, Jane had passed out in the passenger seat, curled up in fetal position. I would put on country music, usually George Jones or Merle Haggard, as I knew it drove her hip-hop-loving ass up the wall. I just love cruising home with a buzz on, singing "He Stopped Loving Her Today."

Eighteen

THE SQUIRTER

Cocaine Jane was a natural blonde with a coiffed hairdo, creamy, olive skin, and alluring green eyes like a cat. A perfectionist, she had with impeccable hygiene and flawless beauty. She always had the best clothes, shoes, and handbags and was gifted with excellent taste and poise. Cocaine Jane was also a cocaine addict (thus her nickname), which gave birth to her darker characteristics of anxiety, paranoia, greed, and envy.

I found her stunning and talented, but didn't trust her as far as I could throw her, so I wrote her off as trouble and avoided her personal space at all cost.

Never did I dream the following events would unfold.

I felt sorry for her when she was onstage. Cocaine Jane wore boas with long, flowing, rhinestone-studded gowns, but her spine was degenerated like a much-older woman. She claimed to be thirty-seven years old, but struggled with low self-esteem and was constantly battling her age, in spite of her elevated beauty. Recently, she had had her near-perfect lips injected with collagen. Her search for pouty lips left her looking more like she had a fat lip. Cocaine Jane was gorgeous on the outside, but all the cosmetic repair couldn't cover the infectious jealousy that blackened her heart and infiltrated her veins and destroyed any real purity that this physically pretty woman might have had at one time.

Cocaine Jane was drawn to me like a moth to light. I was like a butterfly flitting around the club, accumulating cash from every patron I landed on. She knew I was smart but naïve, and she hated having someone as beautiful and innocent as I was doing a better job on her turf.

She became obsessive in her competitiveness. When I had my breasts augmented, she had her breasts done again and larger to match mine. Our relationship reminded me of Cinderella and her evil stepmother. I eventually fell into her trap. She would give me little presents and appear to be my friend. I knew she was as phony as they come; but her tenacity to get next to me exhausted my resistance.

After our day shift was over at 7:00 p.m., I accompanied my scheming colleague to a bachelor party and agreed to entertain with her. We arrived at a small, well-decorated home in Victoria Park. Ft. Lauderdale was all new to me, and it was so much more exciting than the old-folks town of Ft. Myers! I was loving my new environment and was an eager beaver to learn!

Arriving at the party, I was ready to settle in and entertain for a couple of hours, but jacked up as usual, Cocaine Jane didn't waste a moment. She zeroed in on the groom-to-be, laid him on the floor, and grabbed his dick, jerking it like she was pulling weeds out of a garden. It seems as if he was as surprised at his ejaculation as I was!

Jane's eyes darted around the room, alternating between a furtive look of guilt for running in and scamming these men and an artificial smile with batting eyes that she would flash as she was backing out the front door. The group wasn't unhappy; on the contrary, they were chuckling as we departed. Cocaine Jane authenticated the word "trick" in the handbook of a whore. Jane had used me as a prop to entice the men to believe that we were going to put on some kind of sensational show. Obviously, she just took the money and ran.

A couple of months later, another event came up in which a client of Jane's was having his annual party for his mostly Hispanic employees.

This was an all-day affair that paid twice as much as we would have made at the club. I was up for that action!

She drove us to a warehouse district in Ft. Lauderdale at 11:00 a.m., where the office party had already begun. Cocaine Jane was in her usual hyper coked-up state with her eyes darting and shifting, looking like a thief getting ready to rob a bank. I felt as if I was observing a villain in a cartoon. Whom did she think she was fooling?

My jaw dropped when we entered the warehouse workplace. In the center of the room was a mirrored platform with a lanky, strawberry-blond porn star writhing across its span, finger fucking herself. The warehouse was approximately ten thousand square feet, with Ping-Pong tables and coolers full of drinks with scattered desks and work areas.

Bossman John was beaming with confidence and proud of his success and the thriving work environment he had created. John donned an apron and was grilling steak and lobster for everybody. I was comfortably mingling with all the employees, who were drooling over the girls and the food like a pack of hungry wolves. It turned out to be a backroom blow-job kind of day, with yours truly doing most of the work while Jane played madam and pocketed a bankroll and a couple of bags of cocaine.

She offered me cocaine almost like a pusher at times to draw me deeper into her web. I continually refused. This woman was dangerous and on a downward spiral that I was aware of. Being around her in any capacity was risky.

The greed and cocaine caught up to her in the next year. I wound up inheriting Bossman John with more success, more girls, more favors, and more gratitude. In the meantime, Cocaine Jane and I would do a handful of bachelor parties together. Jane would make her grand entrance dressed like a slender Mae West complete with her feather boas as she dripped in jewels and smelled like a French whore. Cocaine Jane was a fast mover. She hated men, or at the very least, her actions toward them. Get in, fake them out, get them off and grab the cash and go! Jane's cocaine addiction was escalating and along with it, her self-destruction.

One afternoon in jealous desperation, she ran into the dressing room screaming, "Persia's sucking a dick!"

I was not doing anything she accused me of; she was just overcome with envy over my youth and popularity and my success over her. One thing that's not tolerated in strip clubs is a catfights!

In her vengeance, she succeeded in getting us both fired.

A month later she called me, lamenting how I had been her only friend and that she wanted any kind of friendship I would give her. I felt her pathetic apology was sincere, but as sick as she was, I could not trust her. Our relationship was over, but from it sprouted a new one with Bossman John.

The following year, he called me to organize his annual company party. His business had grown into an empire of sorts, so he had to be very discreet and handle employees with extra caution to protect his image. The numbers I quoted John raised his eyebrows and made him smile. It made me realize what a greedy con artist Cocaine Jane had been.

I rounded up all my home girls I had a history with, but I needed one more girl to balance the number of men to entertain at the party. I called a friend of mine who frequented the titty bars, and he found a girl for me from the Cat 3. She was a cute, petite brunette and impressively arrived at my apartment on time. I provided a costume for her in reward for her promptness and appearance. A couple of Janes rode together while Candy-Cane Jane and the unknown rode with me. We arrived punctually at the new and well-furnished warehouse with the pack of hungry wolves anticipating their sheep.

Their appetites had grown with their experiences. My posse of pussy was working hard. Bossman John was satisfied, but I demanded an equal amount of compensation for the long hours and workload. This party was rocking!

Bossman John had purchased a longer, wider mirrored stage complete with footlights and a separate room for stage shows. He wanted two of the girls on stage performing at all times.

Ginger Jane and Candy-Cane Jane were in a threesome with the new girl, while Baby-Doll Jane was fucking her with a strap on when whoosh! out gushed a bucket full of fluid from her vagina! The dam had broken; talk about a showstopper. The gush of fluid was not a onetime ejaculation; with multiple insertions, she had multiple orgasms and literally flooded the stage and the room. We were all stunned by this display of waterworks. The phenomenon of squirting was something we all knew of (remember, this was 1996, before the Internet gold rush), but this was a freak show. The crowd oohed and ahhhed with amazement as the small brunette had a crescendo of orgasms, sending waves of watery fluid out of her love lips. The girls were alternating emotions of humor with moments of silence and looks of disgust and disbelief. She quickly adopted the name Squirter.

After each orgasm, she would shudder with emotion and begin to weep. Her knees would buckle if she attempted to stand. We all agreed that nobody in the room had seen such a display of sexual release. The men got a little carried away when they started fucking her with food objects like lobster tails and corn on the cob. The Squirter didn't seem to mind. The other girls were exhausted and grossed out by the fluid. There were no standing ovations—the party was over, and it was time to go home. The girls left with their fists full of dollars, and I wasn't far behind them. I scooped up the wilted Squirter and watched her devour an entire roast beef platter on the way home. This was the beginning of a new frontier for me. To this day, I still wonder where all that fluid came from.

Nineteen

THE STIFF

Life for a stripper wouldn't be complete without getting stiffed—that is, for a dance tip or fee of some kind. In all businesses, you win some, and you lose some. Right?

Maybe it isn't fair to file people into boxes by their profiles, whether it be cultural, racial, or social class, but in my experience, different types of groups exhibit specific and similar behaviors. For example, how many used-car salesmen have you met that don't have a gold-nugget pinkie ring that weighs five pounds?

Well today's lunch-box special person was a pilot named John. Pilots are almost always white-collar guys. They have huge egos and walk around like they all have something equivalent to a war hero's medal. Pilots live fast and are all sex fiends.

Arriving at work one day, I found that the not-so-smart bouncer Scott had been promoted to a managerial position. Peter Principle galore! Fuck! What a nightmare, I thought. Scott was not management material. He started puffing his chest out all of the time and became a total control freak. The last straw for me was when the idiot started hiring only fat black girls. All clubs need variety. This club had a white, Jewish clientele, and an all-black staff didn't work in that atmosphere.

I had had it with this scene and left in the middle of the afternoon. I started driving north, stopping at clubs along the way, looking for the right ingredients, mainly for attractive entertainers. Finally, two hours up the road, I found Club Roxy in Palm Beach. At Club Roxy, the girls were fine! They had tight bodies and pretty faces, and these young things were total exhibitionists on stage. My kind of girls! Perfect for Persia. Girls I could relate to. They also had style and sex appeal. Yep, this club was for me: pretty girls and wealthy patrons.

I met John on a Wednesday. He had just flown in, literally. Pilots were always wild and harried. Perhaps because they fly through the valley of the shadow of death every day, it gave them a certain freedom. John flew for Southwest Airlines. He actually spent money on me in the club, which is a rare thing for a pilot to do. They are usually as cheap as NFL players. I will save that story as another stereotype for another chapter.

Later that night I would get confirmation on what I had learned about pilots in my five-year career. In the meantime, Pilot John laid $400 on me for just a few lame lap dances. My fly guy became a regular customer and would stop by to see me whenever he flew into Palm Beach. I began to think I was wrong to judge Pilot John as a typical egotistical cheap fucker.

"Persia, I would really love to get together with you outside of the club sometime. We know each other now and always have such a good time," John said one night. John was in town for a couple of days before his next assignment. I thought, WTF, he is a good client, understands the game. And I liked him.

"So where do you want to meet, John?"

"How about your house?" he said.

I gave him directions, and we arranged our rendezvous for nine the next evening. I chose a lacy black garter belt ensemble to wear for Pilot John and chilled a bottle of Moët for us. John was a redhead, and if you know anything about them, you know that they fuck like rabbits.

John arrived, and he loved my sexy outfit. We listened to music and drank a little of the champagne. Upstairs we went and had Wild Bill Bronco sex. We sucked and fucked for three hours. More bubbly followed with more sex. What a great session! We started to walk downstairs. Hmmm! I noticed John hadn't left an envelope, protocol for sessions of any kind. I asked demurely, "Did you leave a little something for the maid today?"

"What do you mean, Persia?"

My Persian fuse is short like the rest of me, and I became inflamed at the audacity of Pilot John.

"Is this your idea of a date?" I roared. "You go to a woman's house, drink her champagne, and fuck her brains out?"

Realizing I had been duped and feeling quite foolish, I think I was angrier at myself than at John. Madder than a hornet, I ran into the living room and grabbed the mums that I had in a vase. I lashed out at John and started switching his face with the stems.

"Get out of my house, you dick!"

John had only put his shirt on at this point. Visibly shaken and, I believe, scared at my anger and strength, he reared back his fist to hit me but only had time to grab his pants between switches. Being the multitasker that I am, I managed to grab his only $100 bill out of his wallet before I booted his naked butt out of the front door as he clutched his pants to his chest. I had been stiffed, and all my experiences and beliefs about pilots still stood firm.

Lessons are learned the hard way sometimes. Pilot John taught me that rules of engagement need to be discussed ahead of time. Pilots get so much pussy on the road that it would seem silly for them to donate to such a service. I had a great time gossiping to SPHOS, the aftermath of the memorable switching in my living room. I found mum petals in my living room and dining room for weeks after Pilot John's beating. I might have been stiffed, but the revenge of the moment gave me smiles years later.

Twenty

THE BENJAMINS

Cash is king! I had heard that expression many years before I experienced having any. What cash in my pocket I had in my childhood was lifted out of my mother's billfold. My parents were obsessed with money and were both afraid of losing money and, consequently, were very tightfisted with cash. Let's say that their glasses were always half empty. In short, I got used to the word no.

I married directly out of high school, and my husband was a penny pincher too. It is not so strange that immediately after my divorce, I cashed my hard-earned pension from the hospital and took a vacation to the Bahamas, bought new furniture, and took a job transfer to sunny south Florida.

When I started stripping in 1994, earning cash was like being addicted to a drug. Taking piles of bills home after work was like instant relief of the financial pressure I had been under. Cash was my happiness drug. I would throw it on the bed, then divide it up in ones, fives, tens, twenties, fifties, and good ole Ben Franklins! I became familiar with the smell of money and liked it better than the smell of leather.

I am a hard worker and definitely earned my money. A hustler and thief I am not. Depending on which school of thought you come from,

I am either honest and good or a pushover and dumb. I think most strippers were "hard knocks" kind of girls—child prostitutes often surrounded by domestic violence and poverty that an upper-middle-class girl like me was unfamiliar with. Our family dysfunction was hidden and insidious, only to haunt me in my adulthood. The "hard knocks" strippers stole to survive and had no guilt or second thought about doing so.

Patrons of bars drink alcohol; consequently, their judgment becomes impaired, and they drop money or foolishly spend it or lose it. All employees in bars and restaurants find dollars on the floor and quietly pocket them. One day one of these patrons had done his drinking prior to arriving at the Royal Gold Club. He was a scruffy-looking guy wearing a T-shirt and jeans and carrying a paper bag—full of money. He spotted me and arrogantly said, "Sweetheart, I want you to go get the girl on the main stage and go over there"—pointing to a couch across the room—"and the two of you dance together while I watch you." The dancer on the stage was not one of the most popular girls. In fact, she was one of those "hard knocks" girls who felt victimized by the environment. She would hide behind the columns onstage while she undressed and obviously did not want to be in the club, much less parade around topless, even if her nipples were latex covered. I ran to get her as she exited the stage, explaining to her the gentleman's request. I had told her about the paper bag he had brought in that was full of money. At that moment, I swear, she looked like a cartoon character with dollar signs in her eyes.

We completed one dance and then decided to move closer to him before another stripper grabbed him in his inebriated condition. He was loud, waving his arms and wanting to know how much the Gold Rolls Royce on top of the building cost—because he wanted to buy it! Fuck! He was sloshed! After reaching in his paper bag and giving each of us a Benjamin (a hundred-dollar bill), the dancer I was with locked her claws on his arm and was physically trying to hold him down. I was desperately trying to quiet him and control her greed at the same time.

I wish I was the typical stripper at moments like that. I could yell "Fire!" or "Pussy!" and then grab the paper bag and run like a pig—but hell no! I had to be sweet, honest, and polite, which are three ingredients for a recipe for an idiot with no money to show for it. The greedy slut I was dancing with could not hide her desperation to get the drunken patron's cash. He was smashed on booze and hollering about wanting to buy the gold Rolls Royce on display on the roof of the club.

The three of us had now become a spectacle, and the cocky Italian manager put an end to the raucous behavior quickly. He grabbed the staggering drunk customer by the shirt and the seat of his pants and physically tossed him out of the bar, in spite of the fact that the drunk man towered over him. All I could think was, Motherfucker, cocksucker, whore! I grabbed the manager and said, "Do you realize that slobbering bum had around ten thousand dollars in that paper sack? So what if he wanted to buy the Rolls Royce! He would have spent every last C-note in here!" The manager's eyes became as big as saucers.

Easy come, easy go. For your information, I never asked that girl to double dance with me again. She was like a jinx to me after that incident.

During that same period, another rich opportunity fell into my lap. Behind the main bar of Royal Gold was a U-shaped red booth with a marble table in the center. It was a common place to curl up and get a foot rub from foot fetish customers. I was usually too busy nabbing every man who walked in the door, and I didn't take relaxation breaks. This was long before I learned how to abuse alcohol in the bars.

So on this day, a swarthy, clean-cut gentleman sauntered in and took the right turn to where the bar seats face the open room and the main stage. I was standing at the bar, and we made immediate eye contact. This John did not waste any time. He ordered two drinks and insisted that I give him a lap dance on the U-shaped booth. He started flaunting his money and bragging about how much he had.

I figured out quickly that it was not his money, and he was some kind of mule. From his riddlelike conversation, I gathered he sold weapons for some South American country. At this point, I was turned off and not interested in whom he knew and what he did for a living. He had his own agenda and wanted to take up my time, spacing out the dances and hanging out with me.

Because I was relatively sober and new to the business, this kind of schedule made me impatient and wasted my valuable time. I took a deep breath, leaned back, and tried to endure my time with this loser. My hands were slipped down into the creases of either side of my couch cushion.

On the side next to John, I felt a stack of bills; and I mean a large bundle of Benjamins. I thought for a split second, Fuck! He has no idea that this money has fallen out of his pocket. What kind of asshole wears pants with slanted pockets with that kind of money wad? I could have kept it, but the idea of bad karma and stealing coming back to back to bite me in the ass was gnawing at me. Satan was sitting on one shoulder yelling, "Keep it! Push the stack deeper into the cushions!" Instead, the angel on the other shoulder won the psychic battle, and I pulled out the stack of bills and said, "Lose something?" John's eyes were large and mouth agape.

"Oh, thank you!"

I started scolding him for walking around with that kind of money. He then showed me several stacks of cash that he had stuffed in his pockets. Dirty money for sure, I thought. Okay, but John did reward me—he handed me a new, crisp hundred-dollar bill. What a generous guy! No good deed goes unpunished. Next John!

Twenty-One

The Go-Go Mania

Whew! What a workout! While dancing at Platinum Pussy one day, I was commiserating with a fellow entertainer and relishing the fact that this club was by the far the best for revenue and fun times. She said, "You know, Persia, you might want to go to this club in New Jersey with me next time."

"Yeah? What is the place?"

"The Go-Go Mania, but you have to send a résumé to work there, and they hire only about nine girls per shift." I thought that sounded interesting, and I love a challenge.

When I returned to Florida, I got right on the job. I called the club, got the mail-in info, and two weeks later, the manager Sam gave me a call and said I was accepted and when would I like to fly up. I flew into Newark, and a black Mercedes was waiting for me. The old man brought me to a sleazy hotel that the girls stayed in and tried to talk me into a hand job once we got in the room. I let him grab ass a little bit, then sent him on his way.

I started work the next day at four o'clock. Sam, the manager, picked me and a couple of girls up and then drove five minutes like a bat out of hell to the club. Everybody was silent in the car.

The club was a long brick building of about three thousand square feet. There was an old yellow rollaway marquee out front with unnoticeable black letters, advertising the Go-Go Mania. There was no writing on the building. The floor was brick, and the center of the room had a runway stage with four old-style cash registers, two at each end of the stage that rang up three-dollar drinks. A patron had their choice of Diet Coke, Yoo-hoo, Jolt, fruit punch, bottled water, or O'Doul's. The together in a day was about how much money you could make.

Most of the men drove or trained it down from Manhattan, where the laws didn't allow nudity and lap dancing in the one establishment. The element of sleaze doesn't bother men; they will sit outside for lap dance where you can grab ass and boob at the same time. Most girls got repeats unless a guy was just recently legal age or cash poor. Guys would line up and choose the girls they wanted, and the DJ would then give them a number for that girl. I couldn't believe my ears on the first day when I heard Jerry announce, "Number forty-three for Persia, number twenty-two for Lexi!" This place was a pussy delicatessen.

I was nonstop for the first two hours and told the DJ that I had to take a break. "You aren't going anywhere, Persia. You have ten guys lined up." What an ingenious system! Some men waited up to two hours for a chance to get one of my dances. If an entertainer wasn't dancing, then she would walk around the bar to solicit a dance or do a twelve-minute rotation on the bar stage.

Every girl showed pink, so it didn't take long to build up a string of men waiting for a dance. It was hilarious to hear the DJ continuously yelling out numbers.

After an entertainer finished a dance, he would look in her direction and say, "Okay, Persia." At that point, the entertainer would confirm with the gentleman if he wanted another dance and the dancer would do a lasso like motion over her head, signaling to the DJ to keep the turntable spinning.

One drawback of working at Go-Go Mania was the limited music. The DJ loved hip-hop and didn't give the girls a choice in the music played. Another downer was when you had to sit on the lap of a man wearing blue jeans. It is like boxing without wrapping your hands. Ouch! The upside was getting paid to do nine hours of squats. What a workout! How gorgeous, delicious, and perfect we were.

Women just love to be worshiped and told how beautiful they are. Dancer types in all their narcissism can't get enough attention, so this was a perfect environment to validate their needs. Most of the girls were lovely and just happy to be at this bar, grinding away while making money. Every club has the jealous cunt rat fink who is crotch to crotch with some guy, yawning, hating what she is doing and so busy watching other girls and ready at any moment to accuse them of hand jobs or fucking or whatever to cause problems.

The DJ I had the pleasure of working with was Jerry, an obese young man, expressionless except for his occasional singing and mocking of drum licks from songs he was spinning.

So here was how the system worked: a girl would go into the room to give a dance, the DJ would write her name down. After five minutes, the DJ would push a buzzer. At that point, the patron would have the option to buy another dance for twenty dollars, and the process would repeat itself until the guy ran out of cash or the dancer's nipples fell off. Most girls got repeats unless a guy was just recently legal age or cash poor. Guys would choose the girl they wanted, and the DJ would then give them (check manuscript for missing part).

My three days at the Go-Go Mania were almost over. I caught myself staring at the girls; they were so breathtakingly beautiful. One girl especially, an Asian girl, Tyra, had the most beautiful breasts I had ever seen.

Once back in my hotel room, I showered and felt a horrible stinging sensation on my back. The water really hurt! What was on my skin? Then it dawned on me that I had been leaning up against a shag-carpeted waif while dancing every day and had one hell of a rug burn. The Go-Go Mania gave new meaning to rug burns. I had to smile—the Go-Go Mania rocked!

Twenty-Two

THE SNIPER

My favorite club to work in—bar none—was Platinum Pussy in Memphis, Tennessee! I found out about it from one of the white trash strippers I worked with at Stinkfinger in Florida.

"Persia, you have to go dance at this club in Memphis. You could easily make over a thousand dollars a day!" she told me.

"Memphis?" I asked, surprised. Wow! A successful strip club in my own hometown in the Bible Belt was hard to imagine. I discovered that Platinum Pussy occupied the building that had been the Loft Steakhouse in the seventies. I used to love it when my parents would take me there. The restaurant was decorated like a ski lodge; it had good food leaning toward the expensive side for the times. Now it was still the best establishment—just serving from a different menu, to say the least. It was located on Mt. Moriah at Interstate 40, directly in front of the Piccadilly Cafeteria and conveniently next door to the Holiday Inn. The best part was that it was a five-minute drive to my mother's house. These were great times in my life. I would fly directly from Ft. Lauderdale on Northwest Airlines and arrive in Memphis early enough to work the day shift. My Welsh corgi, Buster, would travel with me. I would drop him off at Mom's and dash off to work.

My shift would end at 7:00 p.m., and many nights I would take Mom out for a lavish meal. She had never been wined and dined or spoiled in life by a man like she should have been, so I wanted to make up for that loss, since I had the means to do it. Mom loved having me around, and since I was working, I could justify staying in town for as long as a month before returning to my home in Florida.

The owner of Platinum Pussy was the only man I ever met who knew how to run a topless bar. He gave the girls freedom to come and go as they needed and had a smile on his face when he greeted them. He always said to me with a thick, southern drawl, "You look real good, baby! Persia, you can dance here any time you want!"

Platinum Pussy was a bottle club, which means they sold setups for people who brought in a bottle of their own liquor. The club also sold beer, and it was so cold it had ice chips in it. Day shift sold two-for-one beer until 4:00 p.m., so we always drew in a nice lunch crowd. The club had massive square footage. Designed in the round, the center stage was in the middle of the room with the tables, chairs, and sofas around the perimeter like a stadium. More chairs and tables were on the east side of the room next to a large stone fireplace that had been left over from the Loft Restaurant. The bar was long, with dark wood and a huge framed mirror behind it; the bar faced the main stage. On the north side of the building was a sunken living room area furnished with about twenty-five comfy couches for the greatest lap dances in the world. The area had several roman columns peppered around the couches, and they were great to hide behind. The area was kept very dark. It was a naughty, naughty place! The other satellite stages were round cages; one was next to the fireplace (I called it the pussy cage), and the other one was in the southwest corner of the club. These were good stages to make tips in, as the men were pussy height if they were standing and watching a dancer. The caged stages also had seating around them, so if a stripper was raunchy enough, she could do an eye-opening floor show and stuff her purse full of dollars afterward. The DJ booth was in the sky overlooking the entire room except for the back room with the couches. A metal spiral staircase was the only access upstairs.

That staircase was not so great for stripper heels or platform shoes to walk up. The entertainer's large dressing-room-and-shower locker area was located on the first floor in the northwest corner of the building.

I just love southern people; they are so friendly and cordial and have a great time in the workplace. Even if they are two-faced and phony, they are still friendly and pleasant to be around.

I was usually the first girl at work. Most of the girls on the day shift were mothers. They would start at 11:00 a.m. and finish in time to pick up the kids from school by 3:30 p.m., leaving with a cool $1,000 in just four to five hours' time. I chose to stay until 7:00 p.m. and many days worked double shifts. The longest shift I ever worked was twenty hours. I was having so much fun that I had to force myself to leave.

I wasn't the only employee who felt that way; one day a couple of managers, a bartender, and a waitress asked me to hang out with them when my shift was done. The employees regularly sat at a table close to the dressing room entrance near the DJ staircase. It was close to the bar as well. I wanted to hang with them, but every time I decided to stop working, I would meet another group of gentlemen who wanted my company. The staff was supposed to go out, but never even left the club.

Platinum Pussy had such a spectacle of people. Stars frequented our club, and it was the only place I have ever seen on the weekends where men and women alike were wrapped around the building waiting to get inside. Nights and weekends had a continuous lesbian act onstage, attracting a crowd about fifteen people deep watching girl after girl get it on with one another.

The DJs were enthusiastic, friendly, and grateful for tips, which was a huge reflection on management. At most other clubs, they were grumpy, demanding, condescending, and burned out. I loved to talk and laugh with the bartender at the beginning of the day. I usually started my day with a cup of coffee and quickly advanced to an ice-cold Coors Light and a cigarette. Nothing like a good buzz before getting naked and sexy on the main stage.

One of those mornings, I asked the bartender, "How do you like my new dress I bought from the costume guy?" His eyes widened, and he said kind of dumbfounded,

"Persia, don't you know who that man is?" I didn't obviously. "That's John. He owns this place and is worth about a billion dollars!"

I hadn't a clue. John was so visible and friendly, and he sold dresses too! No wonder he had so much money.

Today was a normal Thursday in the club. In the southern United States, titty bars attract a different type. I started the day off with Farmer John from Mississippi. He weighed about four hundred pounds and wore big overalls. First man in the place, and he ordered twenty beers immediately. He grabbed me impatiently as I approached and asked, "Where is my girl with my twenty beers?"

"Well sir, it may take her a minute to get all of them on her tray; she is getting them for you," I encouraged. Next, I saw him grab the other waitress and ask her to bring him twenty beers. Five minutes later he had forty beers on his table. I was amused and asked him, "How long is it going to take you to drink those?"

"I don't care, I am staying here all day," he said.

My eyes lit up, and I parked my ass right next to him and danced until every pocket of his overalls was empty. We had a grand ole time together. It was one of those days where I made money early, so I was relaxed and happy, knowing I didn't have to hustle. Things just seem to flow in the right direction with the right attitude. I stayed longer than usual; it was going on 10:00 p.m., and I had made around $3,000. My purse wouldn't hold any more money, so I was going home. Dances were $40 each, and it was like taking candy from a baby!

Right at the dressing room entrance, car-dealer John grabbed my arm, "Persia! I can't believe you are here!" He was from New Orleans and came to Memphis to see his partner once a month. It seems like our trips always coincided.

He was a great-looking young man, around thirty-two years old. He had sandy-colored hair and blue eyes and had perfect features. All he could do was talk about how good looking he was and then ask me if I thought he was good looking. I definitely did, but once I got to know him, I realized how dumb he was, and that really distracted from his good looks.

John pleaded for a dance. "Persia, please don't leave yet. Here is some money; go buy us a beer, and I will tell my buddy that I am coming over to dance with you."

I was tired but consented to dancing for him. I went to the living room area and sat horizontally on a couch that faced the main stage and entrance of the club so John could easily find me. I was sleepily sucking on a bottle of suds with crossed bare legs waiting for car dealer John. I was wearing a black fishnet body suit with a high collar and had on seven-inch black platform shoes.

All of a sudden, I heard a loud pop! Shit! I thought. Someone had thrown a beer bottle at the bar, and there was going to be a fight

The next events happened in seconds. A second pop rang out, the DJ pulled the plug, the club went dark and quiet simultaneously as I watched five hundred people crouch to the floor. Holy shit! There was a sniper in the club, I realized. I watched two black men run past me and out the back door by the kitchen. I thought, What a couple of pussies, but I quickly followed them. I always carried my car keys in my money purse.

Once outside, I looked down at my half-naked body and thought, I can't go home to Mom like this! I ran around to the dressing room door, curious to see what was happening. Now, the nurse in me was coming out, and I went into rescue mode. Several of the dancers at the club were nurses, and we all ended up having nursing duty to do that night. Evidently, a man was in the parking lot roughing up his stripper girlfriend, and the club bouncer kicked him off the property. The man came back with a shotgun and shot the bouncer, filling his arms, legs, and testicles full of buckshot. Ouch!

He was lying in the lobby of the club, bleeding and in shock. I held pressure on his right femoral artery while removing his boot. He was screaming wildly, begging me not to move his legs. He had buckshot splintered through his forearms and calves. The ambulance arrived quickly. Four other patrons had been sitting at a table beneath the lobby's large glass window when the gunshots ensued. The frosted window had shattered on top of them. The other nurse-dancers were picking glass chards from their bleeding scalps.

I finally got home around midnight. Mom was up watching the news and guess what…the events at Platinum had already been broadcast.

"You are not going back to that place!" Mom insisted.

"Oh, Mom!" I whined. "In Florida, if a shooting had happened at one of our clubs, we would be shut down, boarded up, and outlawed, but in Memphis, we will be open for breakfast."

We went to sleep and in the morning, I was right back at Platinum Pussy, drinking a beer and dancing my heart out. Something dawned on me about the night before: If car dealer John had not interrupted my leaving the club when he did, I would have been in the parking lot while the shooting occurred. I guess I was at the right place at the right time after all!

Twenty-Three

Russian Tea Room

John liked his vodka. He had two screwdrivers every evening, then he switched to Miller Lite beer. John liked his women too, fast cars (Cadillacs were his first choice), and he was one driving mother jammer! John really liked his money and had lots of it, but his tastes were on the modest side except for the private jet he owned and that he often flew in.

We met one afternoon on a golf course through one of his employees whom I had been friends with for many years. He arranged a golf game, and I had no idea that I would be meeting his boss.

By his down-to-earth demeanor and his regular-guy appearance, I would not have believed that John was a billionaire. He was so subtle that I didn't even know he was hitting on me! He invited me to his room for drinks that evening.

We had drinks, and he jumped my bones without hesitation. Knowing that the pussy was not for free, John proposed an arrangement and told me that he would like to see m on a regular basis. He traveled to south Florida for business a couple of times a month and wanted me to accompany him on his other business trips.

It was the beginning of a fun-filled affair that would last over four years. John had the most regular schedule of anyone I have ever met; you could set a clock to his routine, and he would eat, drink, shit, shower, and shave at the same time every day.

Like I said earlier, John had his own private jet. He flew me commercially and would usually just call a day or two ahead and let me know our next destination. John always had the presidential suite reserved for us. Our hotel rooms were essentially apartments. John would arrange massages for us most of the time in our suite and without fail had a list of escorts we could call in the prospective city we were visiting. Like clockwork, we had a car (usually a stretch limousine) pick us up at 7:00 p.m., and we would dine at the best restaurants in town. After dinner we would go to different clubs or bars or just go back to our room and call a hooker to play with.

During the day, John had meetings or conventions to attend. I would go play golf at the local country club or golf course, where John had games arranged for me. I could go shopping or do whatever I wanted, but he expected me to punctually be ready to go to dinner at seven sharp. One time I got carried away drinking and playing in a fun weekend tournament at a club in Alabama, After the tournament, all the players including myself were drinking Captain Morgan rum and having a chipping contest off the balcony onto the chipping green down below. I ended up being almost an hour late and quite drunk when I arrived back at our room.

John was not happy with my tardiness *or* the drunken state I was in. Once we got in the limo, he bent me over his knee and blistered my ass red. He was quite a domineering male even though he was affectionate toward me, As I said, John and I had an arrangement and were not lovers; we were more companions. I met lots of his needs and was a submissive enough female for him to keep company.

Before our dinner hour, we would turn on the news and have a screwdriver or two then get in our car and take off for the evening. John was a staunch conservative Republican. I was much more liberal in my views, and we agreed just to disagree on most social issues. Fiscally, we agreed.

John was very gregarious and was always very flirtatious with the waitresses or any female staff at the hotels. He was always trying to pick up pussy for us to play with later in our hotel room. John insisted that I answer the door naked when we ordered room service. It made me uncomfortable at first, but I became accustomed to entertaining his sick sense of humor and kind of liked anticipating the reaction of the staff. They would either act like my nudity was a normal state without any change in facial expression, or they would blush, act surprised, or sometimes just stare.

John reveled in showing me off and loved what a good sport I was. He put me in charge of dealing with all the hookers he would summon to our room. Most of the girls were hags, and we never got the beauties whose pictures were advertised.

They would enter our room and we would give them a gift. Once we wanted to have sex, they would demand a larger gift. I got so sick and tired of these whores trying to extort money out of John. It got to the point to when I answered the door to greet a hooker, I would say, "Unless you are going to eat my pussy and suck his dick, you can leave before you enter this room." That usually put an end to the bullshit the girls tried to feed us.

It was a beautiful July day when I met John in Chicago at the big Marriott Hotel downtown on Michigan Avenue. John had the governor's suite reserved for us. I always had my own bedroom. John and I always played together in his room, but would sleep separately in our own rooms. We were having such a good time on this trip. One of John's idiosyncrasies was for me to give him a bath, manicure, and pedicure on arrival and whenever he requested during our visits. He liked me to groom him at least every other day. John got a little wild while I was bathing him on this trip. He insisted that I service him anally with my fist. I had never done that and was impressed how much fist fucking he could take and how much he liked it. I guess he was more of a pro than he appeared to be.

After an excellent meal at one of the newer restaurants just off Michigan Avenue, John wanted a call girl to come over, naturally. What a surprise! A beautiful Russian trollop showed up and had a delightful way about her. John really liked her. She was a slender blonde with perfect sized C-cup breasts, a stunning face, and a perfectly proportioned figure. He even wanted to have intercourse with her, which was a rare occurrence. She was drinking white wine and drinking too much too fast. I casually asked her what she had eaten that day. "Oh, I had some yogurt this morning for breakfast," she giggled.

"Is that all you have had today?" I asked. John interrupted and asked me to give her some of the Dramamine he always traveled with.

"Dramamine! No way! That is going to make her much worse or pass out!" I told him. He kept insisting, but I refused his request. No wonder he wanted to be fist fucked, I thought. He was probably loaded up on Dramamine himself. I had taken it once as a kid; it was for suppression of motion sickness.

I didn't participate in any sexual activity with our Russian girl, but was an observer. After they fucked, John wanted me to take her to my bedroom and keep her there and take her shopping in the morning. He wanted her again for the next evening. John had a smile on his face and went off to bed as I took the drunken whore to my room.

Fantastic! She started puking all over my bathroom as soon as we arrived. I called room service and ordered hot tea and rolls to get something in the poor girl's stomach. After cleaning the bathroom and giving her a shower, I shoved some tea and rolls down her throat. I was telling her to get to sleep and that we were going shopping in the morning. The Russian insisted that she call her madam and that she needed to leave. I told her she was in no condition to go out and that it was much too late; besides, my man wanted to give her a bunch of presents and wanted me to take her shopping the next day. She would not listen to me and I ended up giving her cab fare and sent her on her way. Good fucking riddance!

The next morning, I explained to John what had happened and that is was a good thing that we did not give the girl any Dramamine on top of all the alcohol that was in her system. John look disappointed and said, "You know, honey, I think I am going to call my pilot and fly on out of here." I told him that I would go ahead and leave as well, after I went down to Marshall Field's and sized the watch he had bought me. John left quickly. It was about ten o'clock. Since the stores were open, I decided to go to the store right after John left.

I walked down to the busy lobby, and what did I see? The Russian whore, her madam, and a Chicago cop huddled in a circle, having a discussion. I thought I was going to pass out at that moment. My pulse started racing, and I had a surge of adrenaline like I had never had before. The light-orange T-shirt I was wearing turned dark orange from perspiration almost instantaneously. I felt like a neon sign, with my DD breasts prominent in my wet T-shirt. I slipped through the revolving door of the hotel onto the sidewalk, hyperventilating and trying to process that the Russian whore was obviously trying to extort money out of my beloved John. How many times do I have to say, "I told you so!" before he believes me about these kind of girls?

Without hesitation, I called John on his jet and told him the scenario going on in the lobby of the hotel. I was sure he knew plenty of people in Chicago to call. I kept walking to Marshall Field's and finished the task at hand to get my watch sized. As I walked back, my pulse started to slow down, and I stopped sweating. I had decided that if the whore was still in the lobby, I was going to approach them and explain the events of the night before.

We hadn't done anything wrong. As a matter of fact, we had helped her and at least fed her when she was sick. When I walked into the lobby, it was business as usual. I went to my room, called the bellman, and left for Chicago O'Hare airport. I am sure the Russian Tea Room in New York was a better experience than ours in Chicago, but it was a good lesson for this John.

John and I continued our escapades for a couple of years longer, but staying more on the golf course and less in the bedroom with strange women.

Twenty-Four

Guido The Few, The Proud, The Cute, The Adorable

Guido. Is that his real name, you might ask? Yes, it is, and don't ask him twice or he might just get in your face. Guido is the only person in this book whose name has not been changed, because he is the only one without baggage. He is probably the most comfortable person in his own skin I have ever met. He stands six foot two, with legs like an oak tree—and by the way, he is very proud of his legs and loves to show them off by wearing shorts. Being Pisces born, he is a natural swimmer. He has straight, thick, black hair, and a goatee that became salt-and-pepper and then gray with age gives Guido a distinguished look. He is remarkably young looking, without a wrinkle or furrow anywhere on his face, which I contribute to his conscious effort not to marry or have children. His nickname is No-No for his dark side; that sums up his highly intelligent, sociopathic side, which is disgusted with the simpletons of the human race. He was Brooklyn born and raised, Jesuit educated. A US Marine. Guido and I are two deviant peas in a pod, free spirits who refuse to do "normal." Never have, never will. We appreciate the avant-garde, the secretive sexy stuff, the things everyone thinks about, but only people like us ever really do. When I say or do something naughty or off the cuff, Guido laughs his laugh and tells me I am "demented," all the while loving my deviant ways.

Guido is a printer, graduating with a degree in political science and went to the printing school in New York. He is like a walking history book and can discuss world issues and history with great rationality and reason, cutting through all politicians' personal agendas and platforms. I would bet on him on *Jeopardy* too if he were to ever appear on the show.

Royal Gold was a bar full of characters, and Guido was one of them. I steered clear of him, as he was there for the drinking experiences, not to waste his money on frivolous dances. Little did I know that Guido and I had a common interest: Tainted Jane.

My new girlfriend, Tainted Jane, was always snuggling up to Guido, who sat at the west end of the bar close to the front door. I generally stayed away from barflies that just sat and drank and didn't appear to get dances or spend money. As I became more experienced and more of an alcoholic, I learned that sometimes just hanging out and drinking could get a girl just as much money.

For the life of me, I could not see Jane's attraction to Guido. He was loud and had that obnoxious Brooklyn twang that I was not accustomed to, being raised in the mid-South.

We came face to face on a Sunday. Just about every weekend, Jane and I would get up at the crack of dawn and start hunting for new treasures at garage sales. Tainted Jane had a Jeep that she loved, and her Taurus moon gave her the ability to remodel and decorate her house for about thirty-five dollars or less every weekend.

"Where in the world are you going to put that sofa and screen?" I would ask. "Your apartment is already jammed full!"

Jane would curl her luscious lips into a mischievous smile and flash her twinkling hazel eyes at me in a seductive way. "Oh Persia, I know just where I am going to put them," she would cry.

I was always amazed how she could rearrange everything to fit like a puzzle and make it look like a work of art. Outside of the club, I had not seen Guido. Tainted Jane spent a considerable amount of time chatting with Guido in the bar. Later I found out that all the gold bracelets, earrings, and ankle chains were Guido's gifts and decorations.

One Sunday, Tainted Jane had purchased too much furniture to stuff into the Jeep. She made a phone call to Guido, who got us a van and hauled the furniture back to her apartment while she finished shopping.

In our small talk, I realized that Guido and I were both sleeping with Tainted Jane. Book smart I was; street smart I was not. My new friend from Brooklyn would not only change that, but become my mentor in the school of life."

Fair-weather friends come and go, as Tainted Jane did. Once she disappeared, I never expected to see Guido again. My run at Royal Gold lasted one year, then I moved out west to one of the sister clubs called Stinkfinger. Lo and behold, in walks Guido. This club was located in his neighborhood in Sunrise, Florida. It was warming to see a familiar face from my best memories at Royal Gold. I rushed to his side, loudly kidding him by pouting. "Where is my jewelry?" Guido had come prepared to seduce someone, because at that moment he produced a heavy yellow-gold bracelet. The surprise left me speechless for a couple of seconds. That was the beginning of a long, endearing friendship.

My first attraction to Guido was the obvious gifts he always filled his pockets with. Second was his deviant and "demented" mind, very similar to my own. Guido and I didn't do "normal"—never had and never would.

Besides a few times together in the bar each week, Guido enticed me with limo rides to Lucky Chang's (a tranny dinner theater that used to be down on Lincoln Road in Miami) or Saturday night fetish parties once a month. I was so proud of this big marine who had a sick sense of humor as I did and was totally secure with his male ego and esteem without a homophobic bone in his body.

Guido's free spirit took me back to the mid-seventies, when I used to hang out with a bunch of gay guys and take off to New Orleans for long weekends of debauchery. Guido was always in the background there for me and experienced lots of good times with many of my stripper girlfriends. I feel like in those days that he wanted one of us to be his girlfriend. I think he finally gave up on me as a marriageable prospect. Our relationship went the distance and was like a cactus with many flowers.

Flowers! Did I mention flowers? Guido showered me with dramatic bouquets delivered on Mother's Day, Valentine's Day, birthdays or just because he was thinking about me—huge arrangements with birds of paradise, orchids, and roses.

Our limousine rides were many, with champagne and vodka flowing all the time. Soon I acquired a couple of nicknames from Guido: Little Persia when the character Farina performed "Little Persia" on the *Little Rascals*. My other nickname, spoken in sarcasm, was Blondie. I have never been a good drinker, possibly due to some Irish and American Indian blood in me, but Guido was quick to remind me when I was having a "blond" moment by saying sharply, "Whatever you say, Blondie!"

Guido has a great laugh that kind of sounds like a loud Popeye. We both have big voices and talk loudly at all times. One of Guido's favorite lines (which he says often when we are together) is, "Who's better than us?" And I would always come back with "Nobody!"

As our friendship grew, our limo days advanced to traditional side trips to New York City. Being the incurable romantic that Guido is, his other nickname is Pepé, named after Pepé Le Pew, the cartoon skunk who was a pussy hound in the first degree. Guido too was a dog who loved the ladies.

Guido started a tradition of booking biannual trips for us on my birthday, September 27, and his birthday, March 16. We went in style, naturally, staying at the Waldorf Astoria and only in the tower suites. We always had champagne and had elegant dinners at various restaurants in Manhattan and Brooklyn. It was great fun walking or cabbing to all parts of the city.

Guido wanted to share every memorable place he had ever been. One of those places was Katz's, which has the best and biggest deli sandwiches in the whole world. Experiencing the city with a New Yorker was incomparable to any other traveling experience in my life. People from the Big Apple know how to take a big bite out of life, for sure! New Yorkers love their city and rightfully so. It's probably the best-built city in the world; the structures are magnificent—the theaters, parks, museums, and sidewalks were built with love and dedication by a melting pot of immigrants whose thirst for a free identity and statement of American nationalism continue to prevail.

Guido rarely went anywhere without his Canon camera. He is a photographer who can catch a smile, a look, or a moment of truth. Guido's best talent is his photographic eye. Being the exhibitionist that I am, I was the perfect subject for Guido to practice on in public. On one of our trips, which happened to be on St. Patrick's Day, we were walking down Fifth Avenue and were talking about how we loved books and what a great pastime reading is. Guido then discovered I had never been to the public library in New York; "You have never been to the libary?" he asked, astonished, in his nasal, Brooklyn accent. That is not a typo; even though Guido was well read, you can't take the Brooklyn out of the boy.

"When it was cold outside, this is where I used to go to play hooky— the public libary!" he told me. Then we were off on an excursion to the public library on Forth-second Street. Up the steps we went past the large stone lions. The architecture was fantastic, with gilded ceilings and marble steps. I was in awe. We wandered into the main room with rows of oak desks, each with a green student lamp and a person studying diligently under each one. Even though the room was full of people, you could hear a pin drop it was so quiet. I found myself walking along the perimeter, gazing at the endless bookshelves and checking out the Dewey decimal system posted on each shelf.

As I scanned one shelf, one particular book caught my eye titled: *The Question of Persia.* The book was published in 1889. Guido had come over and was reading over my shoulder. The author had written how most people don't appreciate the country of Persia. As I flipped through the pages, I saw a photo of a beautiful redheaded woman smiling into the camera with a large, limp white cock in her hand; she had red painted nails and a cum shot clinging to her chin. She ironically resembled Ginger Jane. Guido and I looked at each other in disbelief! How appropriate for Persia to find a sex photo in a book about the history of Persia! Talk about foreshadowing. The moment was unbelievable, hilarious, and just short of perfect.

I can be very abrupt and candid most of the time, but in the early days, Guido would make remarks that could even surprise me and make my jaw drop. Guido and I both were old enough to remember New York in the seventies. I had only been to New York once as a girl before all the good times with Guido. The memories of the trip are still imprinted on my brain. The cabbies back then were almost like tour guides; but one also had to be careful and not get ripped off, as pricing and rates weren't regulated in those days.

Nowadays, almost every cabbie was from India or Pakistan. Guido would land in the cab and call every driver Habib. "Okay, Habib, how about turning the radio down and getting off your cell phone while you drive?" Guido would say.

On a very memorable evening, Guido and I had been to the Village to go to the show *Janis,* Janis Joplin's life story. Guido had seen her get a buzz on and sing "Me and Bobby McGee" more than once, so going to a show about Janis and hearing some of my favorite songs was a real blast!

We were tired after the show and ready to go back to our comfortable suite at the Waldorf. Guido hailed a cab; I fell onto the backseat, and much to my relief, the cabbie was white-skinned for a change. I never let an opportunity to express myself go by. "Thank God, an American!" I exclaimed with glee. The cabbie snapped his head around and angrily yelled in a thick accent, "I am not an American. I am a Russian! I am a molecular scientist!"

I was mortified and amused all at once. Guido being the New Yorker he is with the quickest wit said, "Yeah, buddy. That's why you are driving a cab!" Then Guido mumbled something about wanting to blow his head off. We started giggling between ourselves like a couple of kids in school. Me and my big mouth!

A couple of cab rides later, Guido and I got fed up with another cab driver and hopped out at a bar called the Joshua Tree. We had such a good time there; it was one of the spontaneous memories that cements a friendship. We were with a group of people and had just enough designer drugs onboard to have a great buzz going.

Everyone had just ordered a fresh cocktail, and we were all standing around and talking. Guido's best friend leaned on the table, and all the full drinks were sliding off. I was watching this like it was a slow-motion film; I quickly caught every glass in my fingers in midair and let the table crash to the floor. We all laughed and continued our party. After that night, whenever we passed the Joshua Tree in the future, we would yell to stop the cab and get out and have another drink and toast our good times.

Guido was a boyfriend and at other times a brother; he was always my protector in whatever role he needed to play on that particular day. Our New York memories are the best ones. In March 2001, we decided to take my son with us and go on a "family" vacation. My boy was eleven years old and loved to ride his skateboard. All of our New York trips included a day visit to the World Trade Center for espresso and a photo op overlooking the city and Guido's beloved Brooklyn Bridge. Guido took great pictures of times spent at Liberty Park, the streets of New York, and our moments at the restaurant, Windows on the World.

This particular time, I was commenting on how magnificent the structures of the World Trade Center were. I said to Guido, "This may look funny, but I want you to lie on your back on the sidewalk and set the angle of this great tower straight up!"

Guido was happy to grant my request and took inspiring photos of the building from the ground up. Little did we know that in less than six months, the building and spot we were standing on would be reduced to rubble by the most heinous act of terrorism the United States would ever experience.

Guido always booked our trips ahead of time, and our trip for September was booked to leave on September 14, 2001. Guido asked me if I wanted to cancel the trip. "Absolutely not!" I answered. "I refuse to be terrorized by these cowards." We went to New York on a large jet that had maybe fifty apprehensive people onboard. It was another memorable trip, but full of sadness and grief.

My friendship with Guido continues to grow. It is perpetual and fertile and has all the ingredients that one could ask for in a true friendship: loyalty, respect, and unconditional love.

"Who is better than us?" Guido asks me.

"Nobody!" I answer with a big smile.

Twenty-Five

STURGIS

still haven't figured out if I am more fearless or naïve. Whether it is bravery or stupidity, it makes for good stories and storytelling. Here is one for the ages and for people who love spontaneity.

Sapphire Cabaret was a Ft. Lauderdale club that I danced at for a grand total of two weeks. The place just never worked for me; it was sleazy and wired with cameras in every corner. In a strip club, that mix is like oil and water. Another drawback was that the place drew a crowd only very late, and it was a bunch of barely legal young men looking to get drunk who had no money in their pockets.

In spite of the failure of the venue, one day a long-haired guy with grayish blue eyes strolled over to me and latched on to me quickly. He looked to be in his forties, was tall, slender, mildly handsome but oozing charisma. John had his gray-streaked brown hair pulled back in a ponytail. John spent only about thirty minutes with me, but in the short time was enthusiastic and had an unusual and enticing proposal.

"Persia, do you like to ride motorcycles?"

"Well, my first love was a motocross fanatic, and many of the boys and girls I grew up with rode motorcycles, so I have experience on the back of a bike." I answered.

"Have you ever heard of Sturgis?" John asked.

"No. What is Sturgis?"

"It is the biggest and best bike rally in the country. It is located in South Dakota. I would really love you to go with me. It takes place in August."

I was flattered and surprised to meet someone and to be invited on more than a casual trip. John was going on and on about the beauty of South Dakota and what a fantastic time he always had out there. He promised that if I went with him, I would have the time of my life and never forget it. John went on to say how I would be thanking him forever for such a great time. In the same breath John said, "Persia I have to get home. My girlfriend is pregnant, and I can't stay out late."

Instantly I felt huge disappointment that John wasn't single. He wasn't the typical guy who went to strip clubs. He was with a buddy, so they had a quick stop at the bar for a happy hour cocktail before going home.

"Persia, I want you to buy a ticket flying to Rapid City on August seventh through thirteenth. I will reimburse you when we meet there," John said.

"Is there a club I can dance at out there? I can't afford to take that much time off work," I answered.

"Yes, Wet Willie's is a great little bar, and you would have lots of patrons from the bike rally," John encouraged. Then John dashed off and left me sitting there under his spell.

I gave his proposition some thought over the next week and took the plunge and bought a round-trip ticket from Ft. Lauderdale to Rapid City. It was only May, and when August rolled around, I started mentally scolding myself for getting sucked into John's game. I picked up the phone on August 5 to cancel my ticket when my cell phone rang. I was astonished to hear John on the other end saying, "Are you ready to go to Sturgis?" he asked cheerfully

"Well, yeah, as a matter of fact I am," I stumbled, disbelieving the coincidence of the call. I don't know who was more surprised, John or me.

John continued to go into detail about the weather and that I would need a leather jacket, gloves, and chaps to ride. He told me that he would have a limousine waiting for me on my arrival to Rapid City.

I was nervous on the plane. John and I had met only once. Would I remember what he looked like? God! What did he look like? I was doubtful and now was regretting my impulsivity. Would I ever control or outgrow acting without thinking?

I loved the western part of the country. The view out of the airplane window over the Badlands tugged at my heartstrings and brought back memories from my childhood, when I had traveled with my family all over this part of the country. My heart was about to beat out of my chest when the plane touched down in Rapid City. I was wearing blue jeans, a white T-shirt, and my black Harley-Davidson boots. After leaving the gate, I walked down the corridor with searching eyes and spotted John on the left side with the same anxious look on his face, as if he wouldn't remember what I looked like. I felt apprehension as I smiled at him, and I knew he sensed it.

My facial expression might have led him to believe that I was disappointed in his looks. John had gray eyes and long, gray-streaked, brown hair he wore in a ponytail like a middle-aged wannabe Hell's Angel. Even though his physical appearance was stereotypical, his personality was not.

He had invested money as a young man and put it in offshore accounts. He was smart, private, goal-oriented, and knew what he liked. He loved motorcycles and was impressively knowledgeable about their parts and functionality. Our eyes met, and once we got past the uncomfortable reacquaintance to one another, we walked out of the airport to our week-long adventure.

John had told me he would have a limousine waiting for my arrival. Proud and pleased, I saw the black stretch limo ready for service at the curbside. It was probably the only limousine in Rapid City. John threw my bags in the opened door and slammed it shut. "Aren't we getting in?" I asked. "Oh no, sweetie. We are taking the Road King to the Alex Johnson Hotel," John replied.

His black Harley was parked in front of the limo. "Hop on, Persia," John commanded. Breathless and openmouthed, I nervously asked, "Where is my helmet?"

I had grown to hate motorcycles from my many years of experience working in the ICU and emergency room. The hospital personnel cynically called them "murdercycles."

"They don't have a helmet law out here in South Dakota!" John exclaimed.

Oh, hell no! I thought. I got on the back of the Road King and wrapped my arms tightly around John's slender waist. I felt my knuckles turning white. I sheepishly whispered trying not to show my anxiety, "John, can you slow down a little?"

"No way, Persia! This is what gets my dick hard!" he yelled above the wind.

What the hell had I gotten myself into? At that moment, I regretted ever meeting John.

It was a sunny, crisp day around sixty-five degrees. The mountain air, blowing all around us, was invigorating. The ride to the Alex Johnson Hotel was about thirty minutes. What a beautiful place! I felt like an actress in an old Western movie minus the hoop skirt. Well, apparently John was a man of his word. He did get a limo and had the honeymoon suite with a heart-shaped Jacuzzi in our room. He was sexy as hell too, and the ambiance of our room ratcheted up his sex appeal a couple of notches. We toasted with champagne upon arrival to our hotel room, and John couldn't wait to get my clothes off and fuck. John had a foreskin, and it really enhanced our stimulation during intercourse.

Oops! He lasted an entire two minutes! After his premature ejaculation, he had to call his "wife." He wasn't formally married, but had lived with his woman for eight years. They had a seven-year-old son and now a three-week-old baby boy. When I realized he had left his wife and newborn to take a trip to Sturgis with me, I lost all respect for John and couldn't stop thinking about it for the rest of the trip.

From the first phone call he made, I felt like a home wrecker. The situation was doubly disappointing because here I was in a romantic scenario with a strange man I felt very attracted to, and he was essentially unavailable. Fortunately, the trip came with distractions. John had friends and acquaintances along for the rides we went on. Off we went to cruise on the bikes.

Over the next three days, I developed a numb and almost callused rear end. Our group consisted of four bikers. We traveled to Mt. Rushmore, the Badlands, the towns of Deadwood and Lead, and the Crazy Horse and Devil's Tower monuments. While touring the museum and the Crazy Horse monument, John said, "Let's take the helicopter ride around the monument!" Words can't do justice to the size and magnificence of the structure. Mt. Rushmore pales compared to the Crazy Horse project.

John and I fell in love slowly and surely. After all the riding, it took a few days to relax, take it all in, and get the color back in my hands. I had never ridden for an extensive time on the back of a bike. A three-day ride is totally different from an afternoon cruise on a bike. I saw so many things and noticed details that I might have missed if we were traveling by car—such as a funeral home on the curve of the main street in Deadwood named Caput Funeral Home. There were lots of hills, curves, and mountainous terrain all over this state. Whenever I expressed any fear, John would look at me and say, "Honey, I haven't laid a bike down in twenty-five years, and I am not about to now, not with you on my bike and a new baby at home."

Harleys are so goddamn sexy too! I wrapped around John with my legs spread, the bike vibrating, and smelled his hair and leather jacket in my face. I loved feeling his body, and I knew he was melting into mine with every tight embrace. We stopped at a neighborhood kids' lemonade stand. There were small, spring-fed creeks with wildflowers all around them and fields full of prairie dogs. We stopped to climb on big rocks and take photos. We ate rainbow trout almost every day.

John became more and more protective of me. He finally did take me to Wet Willie's topless bar as he had said he would do, so that I could work while I was away from home. John wasn't about to let me dance in this biker joint. "Baby, I will give you money to pay your bills, but you are with me now," he said while escorting me outside.

We spent only one day riding to Sturgis. The ride on Highway 85 was poorly lit and downright scary. Once at the bike rally, the scene was total carnage. Everybody was sporting tattoos and bare asses hanging out of leather chaps, and they were drunk and acting like fools. I saw people so hammered they were falling off bikes that were sitting stationary on the main drag. It was a perfect element for the exhibitionist in me, but my new lover couldn't stand it and rushed me back to our honeymoon suite to make love and keep me all to himself.

I found myself waking up with a love glow every morning. John felt it too. He was romantic and generous with our lovemaking.

The last day of our trip had come too soon. We rode alone to Wyoming and walked around Devil's Tower. I went shopping at a Christmas store out in the middle of nowhere. We rode until dusk, when the air started to cool through my leather. I could feel John's sadness that our vacation was at an end. He had fallen harder than I had and was careful not to kiss me too much or get carried away with our unexpected intimacy.

John put me on the plane the next day. His farewell was brief. He was right about one thing: I would remember this trip forever and thank him for one of the best times of my life.

John and I continued to see each other after Sturgis, but he turned out to be a better husband than I thought he was. He couldn't love us both, and without even a discussion, we both knew the inevitable that John belonged his with his wife and children, and our romantic fling had come to an end. Next!

Twenty-Six

The Stalker

It was the week before Thanksgiving. There are certain times of the months and year that are the worst for bars. Naturally, the beginning of the month when the rent or mortgage is due is a shock to the pockets, so nobody had any fun money for a lap dance. Mother's Day was another day they might as well be closed, as all were taking their mothers or mothers-in-law to brunch whether they wanted to or not, but the year-end holidays were about the worst time. Men aren't great shoppers, but most of their holiday activities were obligatory to employees or families, and that left little time to hang out in a titty bar.

This particular November day, the bar was like a tomb. The staff and entertainers were all bored, and on the quieter days, I lost motivation fast. In walked a John who came over to the back of the bar facing the stage, where the small bunch of us were seated. He was six foot one with a dark complexion. His hair was dark with a receding hairline. Mesomorph-like, he was half beefcake and half chubby, like an ex-athlete that still ate like one. This John had a girl's name, which was appropriate for this man, as I found out much later.

John was charming enough. He was a talker and a smoker and had one of those signature raspy, gruff, loud laughs. I obliged him to a couple of dances and intuitively sensed something cheap about him. John hung around the bar for a couple of hours, buying drinks and bought a couple of more dances before he predictably hit on me. He invited me to a Thanksgiving party he was having at his condo down in Miami, one of the high-rises off Biscayne Boulevard. I decided against it and turned down his invitation.

I got home at 8:00 p.m. after work. Within minutes my phone was ringing. John had managed to charm me out of my phone number that evening, and it looked as if a courtship had begun. Prince Charming talked my ear off until 11:00 p.m. I let him get his foot in the door and accepted his second invitation to a sushi restaurant later that week. The sushi date was just okay—no spark, no magic. My son was invited as bait for the kind of predator type this man turned out to be. Intuitively, I felt uncomfortable with this John. I should have seen the writing on the wall. My little son's body language showed me that he didn't like him either.

One would think that at forty years old, I would have had enough life experiences not to become vulnerable once again. I guess my breakup with Fat John had affected me more than I realized. Even though it hadn't been real love, just the adoration and the security of having Fat John and his family around was enough for me to deny, put on blinders, and set myself up for the biggest brain fart of my life!

I got sucked in fast. I started driving to Miami three times a week to see John. You see, he was on probation for DUI and had a driver taking him to work. We lived thirty minutes apart, and it was more convenient for me to drive to him.

It is almost unconscionable that I didn't dump this John immediately. As much as I had learned about alcoholism, and here I was dating another drunk. One night he was to speak at an AA meeting, so I agreed to go with him. I had been to lots of these meetings before, and this one was a very strange one. The people in the meeting weren't getting honest or calling people on the bullshit that was spewing out of their mouths, including John's. He embarrassingly professed his love to me in front of the group, going on and on how our love was so phenomenal, and he felt like it had saved him.

That is so-not-healthy behavior, and I think the group was so shocked that they didn't know what to say. It was another obvious sign that I chose to turn a blind eye to.

The next week, John wanted to go to the same meeting, and I wanted to be supportive of him, but I was going to be late to pick up my son from his baseball practice. I was getting angry at this man's interference in my life, so I pulled over, dropped him off on the turnpike, and told him to walk the rest of the way. I was glad I had, as I got back to practice five minutes after they had finished.

The courtship moved quickly, and John asked to move in with me in February. He couldn't wait to get married. The idea of getting married started to grow on me. Too bad I was so efficient with the planning. I pulled it together in three weeks, just as I had my first marriage. We decided to get married at the old church in Coconut Grove. It was a sunny day when I went to sign the contract for the church.

As I was turning onto the street to enter the church, a girl in a car came flying over the hill in my lane. I had to swerve to miss a head-on collision. I had to pull over and stop to keep from passing out. "Was this another sign?" I asked myself. I shook it off and went into the church. The wedding date was set for May 29, 1999.

John and I shopped for a ring and a dress. I bought a beautiful designer dress at a very expensive store on Los Olas Boulevard. John bought my ring from a jeweler in Coconut Grove. It was a two-carat brilliant solitaire diamond—really a beautiful stone.

I invited all my golf buddies and friends. John didn't have too many to invite: just his psychiatrist and a handful of others who didn't show up. My mother arrived the day before the wedding. She met John and videotaped us opening gifts.

"You know, honey, you can always call this wedding off," she said.

"Oh, Mom! I have already paid for everything; I can always get divorced," I replied.

Mom knows how hardheaded I can be, so she didn't push the issue.

My best friend, Jane, showed up the next day. I could tell by her expression that she didn't like John either. We all went down to the Rusty Pelican in Miami for the rehearsal dinner. There were about twelve of us at dinner. John came to me at the conclusion of the meal and asked to borrow my credit card, as his had been rejected. I didn't know if I was more angry or embarrassed. I handed over my card and tried not to cause a scene and embarrass the wedding party.

The wedding was scheduled for 4:00 p.m. The limousine came to pick up Mom, Jane, and me at one. We piled in the car and needed a stretch limo to fit all the lace of the wedding dress inside. As soon as we got in, the skies opened up, and a torrential downpour ensued. The driver headed east on Sample Road and passed I-95 and started driving south on US 1.

"Where are you going?" I questioned. He told me he was driving to Coconut Grove. "Well, if you plan on getting there before Tuesday, then we better turn around and get to I ninety-five!" I told him.

Jane had a pensive look on her face and had her hand around her throat, supporting her chin. She looked so sad to me. We arrived at the church only thirty minutes before the ceremony was to begin. I started to get ready and had a glass of champagne, which would not be something I would do before a serious occasion such as my own wedding. My sister was there, and it was kind of awkward, as we hadn't really communicated in years.

It was supposedly a joyous occasion, and deep in my heart, I felt like a fool on parade. Where was my Shpos, my slut of honor? I felt uncomfortable and started getting nervous like she wasn't going to show up. Shpos, the slut of honor, in all her selfishness finally showed up at the last minute. Jane, my best friend of all time, helped me, but I guess it was more appropriate for Shpos to be the maid of honor in this horror of matrimony. The entire event had a definite undercurrent of uneasiness.

My father's family and second sister attended the wedding. It felt odd, as my family had betrayed and rejected me because I became a stripper years ago. Only because of Doc's encouragement did I invite my family. Forgiveness for them was not available in my heart at that point in time. My father escorted me down the aisle for the second time in my life and very awkwardly gave me away. John looked like a criminal getting away with murder. Nobody liked him.

The soloist, one of my good golf buddies and coworker on the board of the state golf association, was singing like a bird when crack! boom!"—lightning hit the church, and the lights went out!

The preacher said, "There is a message here."

Yeah, I thought—run for my life! I was standing there in disbelief and ruminating about all the signs I had received over the past two weeks. I knew this union was wrong and a mockery of the vows I was about to take. I even thought about saying, "For richer or for richer" rather than the traditional "For richer or for poorer," but held my tongue. Stalker John was so nervous that even the preacher and I couldn't hear what he was mumbling out about. He supposedly had written some special fucking poem, but since he was fumbling around like an idiot and no one could hear a word he was saying, it is still a mystery. He was probably reciting an evil incantation! The wedding ceremony was done in about fifteen minutes once the power came back on. Did I feel relief or regret?

The Tiffany Room at the Mayfair Hotel was a round room with an abstract, swirly design on the carpet in red, black, and purple. I had heard that the food was delicious. Being a typical bride, I didn't have a moment to eat or drink a thing, and nobody thought to bring me anything either. The band I hired was fantastic, and I danced with my sweet, young son, my father, and my new, clumsy groom. I enjoyed seeing all my friends have a good time. John had one guest show up, his psychiatrist.

I caught him staring at me dumbfounded and confused. What the hell was I doing with this guy? That is what his eyes and facial expression were asking. A couple of my older, seasoned golf friends came up to me and commented on what a jackass my father was. He was usually inappropriate and abusive, as my mother and his new wife were both in attendance. In a situation like my wedding, my father's actions would take misogyny to a new level.

I managed to choke down several glasses of champagne. Jane came over to John and me. Before she left with my mother and friends, she sharply instructed him, "You better take care of her!" and then she broke down in tears and gave me a big hug.

I puked after everybody left. Another sign, no doubt. I was sad the party was over. Here I was, just John and me married. Oh God! The food and beverage manager tried to gouge me for five grand for the open bar. All of my friends and family didn't drink alcohol, so John put an end to that scam very quickly.

The party and wedding had cost me twenty thousand in all. When it came time to buy the two-carat diamond ring, John's credit card didn't work, and I had to buy my own ring! I wasn't feeling very good about all of this.

So we flounced out of the Tiffany Room onto the streets of the Grove and rode around in a rickshaw, showing off in an attempt to give the appearance of happy newlyweds! Not! After the spin around the Grove and making a few heads turn, we headed up to the honeymoon suite at the Mayfair Hotel. My tulle-skirted dress was adequately saturated with street soot around the bottom, and John in his tuxedo was handsome but disheveled, as usual, like most chubby men tend to look all the time.

Our suite was maize-and-black-marble throughout. The dining room had a huge, rectangular ebony table that could seat eight guests. The sunken Roman bathtub was just a few feet away from a massive bed. For a couple in love, it was a place to luxuriate and fornicate for days on end.

For me being with John was like being in Alcatraz. We got undressed and had sex out of some kind of obligation. Here I go again, I thought. On my first honeymoon, I cried my eyes out after having robotic-type sex with my husband, which lasted all of three minutes. Sex with John was worse.

I stopped after a few minutes. His dick was small, and he was constantly looking at me with a question of approval. I think John was a latent homosexual. How fucked up was I to marry a doofus like John? He was begging me not to be sad and wanted another attempt at a pathetic sex act. I refused.

The next morning could not come soon enough. We went to the beautiful restaurant and had breakfast. My father and his family were also in the restaurant. Dad pulled me aside and started questioning the credibility of this man I had married;

"Where is his family? He didn't have any relatives or friends at the wedding!"

I had no answer and agreed with my father. Uncomfortable and wanting to crawl under a rock, we ate hurriedly and left to go back to my house in Coral Springs. My father and I hadn't visited in about ten years. The wedding did not break the ice. It was more like shit on top of ice cream.

I was relieved to be away from the scene of the wedding crime and back home to greet my mother and my poor, disturbed son. He hated John too. We all did. I wanted to make the situation tolerable. The next morning, we went to brunch at the country club that we were members of, the Coral Springs Country Club. I was driving my new Q45 Infiniti that John insisted I trade my 328 I BMW for.

"I know this girl at Infiniti who can get us a great deal on a new car. We need more room, and they make such dependable automobiles." Nothing was wrong with my BMW. John just wanted his name on the vehicle. The car was an olive-green color. I hated it.

After Sunday brunch, I stopped at a shopping center to pick up some milk at the store. I always exited on the north side of the parking lot, which had less traffic and a quiet, convenient stoplight, but not today. I drove to the east side of the lot to exit onto University Drive. I stopped in the lot before exiting and turned around to tell my son to make sure that his seat belt was secure. I figured that my mother and John were adults and could take care of themselves. Once I was on University Drive, I slowly took a right turn and headed east onto

Shadow Wood Drive when a small, red Geo came screeching out of the Coral Square Mall.

I saw the car sideswipe two cars in line preparing to exit the mall parking lot. The car was coming fast and heading right for John's door on the passenger side. I slammed the brakes so hard that the car buckled and felt like it was bending in half. The Geo miraculously missed slamming into us and crossed the median, hitting a city bus.

The Geo had lost its front fender and was heading west, going down the wrong side of the street and blowing through the red light that I would have been sitting at if I had taken my usual route. I was thinking at that moment that my angels were really working overtime and really wanted me to get away from John. We were all stunned, amazed, and relieved that we had been spared from an almost disaster.

Mom went back to Memphis the next day. The following day was the beginning of a four-day holiday at the Boca Raton Resort, a kind of honeymoon–family vacation combo, before my son left to visit with his father for the summer visitation. The resort was only fifteen minutes from my house. On the way to check in, John and I got into some argument about a mile from the house, and John jumped out of the car. My son quickly said, "Leave him, Mom!" I gave his suggestion serious thought and then considered that this creep would go back to the house and probably rob me or burn it down. We encouraged dickhead John back into the car and continued with our vacation.

It was mostly uneventful, except for a wrestling match between John and my son that started to get too rough when I loudly put an end to it. John got my dander up again when we were leaving to take my son to the airport. I opted to go alone with the boy, much to my son's relief. "Mom, he is such an asshole!"

I was surprised at the slur against John as my son was very tolerant of people and never called people names even in the worst situations. It made me smile with validation.

John woke up in the middle of the night regularly, usually around 3:00 a.m. I would hear him down in the kitchen, foraging like a bear, eating everything in the refrigerator. The second night of holy matrimony was holy fucking hell for me.

While on his eating rampage, John woke me up in the middle of the night to discuss our relationship.

"What relationship?" I screamed. "We have only known each other four months; how can we have any kind of relationship yet?"

Enraged and at my rope's end with this nut case, I snapped off the stalk of the corn plant outside of the bedroom door and started beating John over the back with it.

"Get out of here and let me sleep!" I yelled.

Thank heavens, John was leaving for Texas the next day to start his new job. I had insisted that John go get himself established in Texas before I sold the house and joined him. Much to his chagrin, he schlepped off to the Lone Star State alone.

Soon after John left for his new venture in Texas, I started receiving all his forwarded mail from his previous address. John was in debt. Not only was he in debt, he was delinquent on several credit cards and owed about $8,000 on his beat-up old black truck. I realized I had gotten myself into a pickle. I immediately called the preacher who had performed our wedding ceremony.

"Mr. Preacher, I was married on May twenty-ninth, 1999, and I would like to annul the wedding."

"Mrs. John, I perform lots of weddings, and normally I can't recall one from another, but I *do* remember your wedding."

I thought, How could he forget it since the wrath of God struck the church with a bolt of lightning!

"Annulment is a procedure in the Catholic Church. Your paperwork has been sent in to the state, so it is out of my hands now." The minister sighed regretfully. "I suggest you check into divorce proceedings."

The next week I was traveling to Texas to our new homestead and planned to play in a golf tournament in Oklahoma, since I was already in the Midwest. When I arrived in Dallas, I pulled up to John's housing unit in my rental car with my Welsh corgi, Buster Nuggets. The place was a prefab, fifty-room dump. Prior to this trip, I had visited with

John's employers, and they all lived in mansions. What was he doing staying in a housing project? The room was small, dark, and dank. John had golf games set up for me at Los Colinas Country Club, Gleneagles Country Club, and also at the TPC course in Dallas. When John would leave for work, I would go to a different golf course every day.

When I returned the first afternoon, there was a sign posted on the door, "No Pets Allowed." Another lie! Poor Buster must have barked and given himself away. John snatched the sign off and tried to hide it before I saw it, but it was too late. I was furious at John. I took the dog to the car with John chasing after me. I drove around the corner and found a park and screamed at John;

"Now what do we do? Where are we going to stay?"

As I drove around, ranting and raving at John, miraculously I found a doggie day care directly across the street from the housing project. It was only five dollars a day. I decided we could drop him off early in the morning and then sneak him in the room in the evenings. I would pick him up from daycare and take him to McDonald's and the park every day. It was like having a toddler all over again.

The third day in Texas, I was home earlier than John and found an open cardboard box with all of John's papers in it. Oh my! His debt was worse than I thought. He had lied about everything and was in severe financial distress. When John got home, and I confronted him about his lies, he grabbed me and hugged me. I was so angry and repulsed, I sank my teeth into the back of his shoulder, biting it so hard that I am sure today he has my teeth marks as a tattoo. It was well over a hundred degrees in Dallas, but I went to bed fully clothed and seething with anger, unable to sleep and never wanting to touch this man again.

I had played three days of golf in Texas and went to a couple of outings his new company hosted. John was obsessively calling me, which I found suspicious and inappropriate, since he was just starting his new job. I called my aunt in Oklahoma and told her that I was coming to her house a couple of days early rather than stay in Dallas with John anymore.

I was shaking with anxiety as I drove down Highway 35 north to Oklahoma City. The anxiety started to slowly drift away the farther I was from Dallas. I told my aunt to observe John when he came to visit for the weekend, but not to discuss anything with me until he returned to Dallas.

I played great golf and won my flight in the tournament at Oak Tree in Edmund, Oklahoma. Once John left, my aunt (who was extremely bright and intuitive) said, "Well, he really seems to love you and appears to be an okay guy."

I expected a different opinion. I felt confused and lost. I returned to Florida on Sunday.

Monday morning John called. "Hi, honey. I have some bad news. I lost my job and I am coming home."

"What? This is my home, not yours. We are getting a divorce"

I yelled hysterically. I slammed the phone down and took a deep breath. I realized that I had to con this con man to maintain my independence and not lose everything. I contacted an attorney and started the divorce process.

I was afraid to call anybody else right away. I was feeling shocked and numb and was trying to organize my thoughts, so I could act rationally.

On Wednesday, my aunt called me. "Persia, I had a bad dream last night, and I think you should get away from John as fast as you can."

"Oh God! I am so glad to hear you say that! He got fired on Monday and wanted to come back to Florida, but I won't let him come back here."

John started calling me sixty to one hundred times a day. He had gone to his sister's house in New Orleans and said he found a job with an old friend in Georgia. I lied and promised to come and be with him soon. I had to placate him and work him as much as possible so that he would pay his bills.

It was mid-July, and I finally convinced him that we must get a divorce. I coerced him with the threat of court, so he unwillingly signed the document. We were divorced in five minutes on September 9, 1999, with the judge granting me $14,000 that John owed me. Of course, I never received a dime!

I celebrated my divorce with old buddy Guido by getting hammered on vodka and cranberry juice at Brownie's (a bar across the street from the Broward County Courthouse).

The Stalker had just begun to spin his evil web. He started calling my friends and family. John's phone calls increased in number to me, if that was even possible. I stopped answering the phone. He threatened my life in a message left on my phone machine, and I got a restraining order against him. He continued to stalk family and friends, trying to alienate them against me.

December of that year, John sent the board of directors of my golf association, my father, and my ex-husband a nude magazine article I had been published in that August. He started telling lies, telling them all that I had webcams and was prostituting out of my house, exposing my son to sex.

Only the executive director of the golf association called me—not my father or ex-husband. She knew it was all a bunch of lies and returned the magazine to me.

My father, on the other hand, got a sheriff's order to investigate my house. My son was to visit his father that Christmas for his holiday visitation. My ex-husband and father kidnapped him, telling him that he wasn't returning home. The boy was devastated. Nothing was found except that the judge was appalled that these two men had shown the boy my website. He ordered the boy returned to his home with me. The men started regular communication with John and pursued their case in the Fourth Circuit Court in good ole Music City USA, where the kangaroo circus began!

Twenty-Seven

The Politician

It was March 2001. My son was away, and the stalker was out of the picture for now. I was finally enjoying some peace and quiet and settling into a consistent schedule at work.

I had written several legislators and congressmen for assistance to battle the Tennessee court system, through which I was being railroaded. Even though Florida was my son's home state—and as hard as they tried, they could not prove me unfit by any standard—they were still taking the boy away from his home.

I had pretty much given up hope on getting any help, and then the phone rang.

What's this? The man at the other end had actually read my letter and hadn't tossed it in the proverbial pile of citizens crying victim. Wow! I was impressed. Politician John listened patiently to my entire story. He followed up by calling me a week later and telling me that his entire staff was working on my problem. I was elated and had visualized a staff of twenty writing letters and making phone calls trying to collect the facts and reveal the truth of this travesty. Even if he had only one assistant, it didn't matter; what mattered was that this man genuinely seemed to care and was willing to help me. John had given me all his numbers and contact information and subtly asked me during one conversation what my website address was. I noticed that his voice was incredibly seductive. After spilling my guts out to this guy, he asked me, "What was your website again?"

"Www.persjaspalace.com," I replied.

"Is this you on the website?" he asked.

"Well' yes," I said.

Politician John asked me a few more general questions about the website before I realized he was masturbating while he was talking with me! At first I was disgusted and disappointed, asking myself, wasn't there one individual in the world with any integrity? Did everybody just want sex or money? Then I just hung up the phone thinking that all politicians were just the scum of the earth.

Politician John started calling regularly—daily in fact. For the record, I had not been in a sexually stimulating relationship in about ten years. John was probing me for phone sex, and I found myself curious and turned on.

"What do you look like?" I asked.

"I have dark hair, green eyes, and I'm six-one." John gave me his website address and told me to go look him up.

"How big is your cock?" I candidly inquired.

"Six inches," John quickly answered.

I immediately ran upstairs to *my* office to look up Politician John and told him that I would call him back. I checked out his profile photo and thought his body looked all right, but he was balding, and his main hobby was bird watching. What the fuck?

I was not turned on, to say the least. Nothing against bird watching, but it was kind of a sissy hobby, and a red flag went up in my brain. Oh, what the hell, I told myself, I wasn't thrilled, but I hadn't been this excited in a very long time. I was going to have some fun with this situation. John started calling me every afternoon, giving me butterflies with his very sexy voice. I told him that I was attracted to him and that I thought he was very handsome. John thanked me and confessed that he was a little heavier since the photo on his profile display had been taken.

"Oh yeah? Just how fat are you?" I questioned bluntly.

"Well, listen to you!" John answered with a long, silent pause afterward.

I blew off getting an answer, since John was so charming. The phone would ring at 3:00 p.m. every day. I would run upstairs, ripping my clothes off as I went. I would jump into bed and take out my favorite vibrating toy. John and I were having very steamy phone sex. John fantasized about me coming to his office, wearing a black suit, white blouse, black stockings, and garter belt. He would get up from his chair, stand behind me, move my hair to one side, and then start softly kissing my neck. John would take his very large hands and gently rub them in downward strokes over my breasts.

At this point of the fantasy, I would get so excited that I would start panting loudly. John would gently command me to remove my jacket. He would slip his hands around my waist, unzip my skirt, and slide it over my bottom letting it fall to the floor. John would then ask me to sit down and return to his chair behind his desk and just stare at me.

After a couple of minutes, John would order me to unbutton my blouse. I would do as I was told while John piercingly stared at my face, telling me how much he loved my big, brown eyes, full, pink lips, and shiny, dark hair. His voice became deeper and softer. "Baby, push your breasts together."

I gazed at him, felt my face redden, and I obeyed him. "Now I want you to spread your legs," John commanded. As I was getting comfortable, John would passionately leap on top of me and ravish my body.

After a month or so of hot phone sex, I was realizing how lonely I was without a lover. I started carrying my cell phone everywhere, and my heart would skip a beat whenever his number would pop up on the screen. I wanted to meet John in person, in the flesh. We had decided to rendezvous at my house one Friday night around six. I was bubbling over with excitement and glee! I waited for his phone call, and waited, and waited. By 9:45 p.m. he hadn't called, and I was pissed! I gave up on him.

At 10:00 p.m. my phone rang. John's number came up on the caller ID. It rang once and then he hung up.

I called the number back and left a message. "If you changed your mind and weren't going to show up, at least have the courtesy to tell me so!"

John called me back and said, "Persia, I'm just trying to do the right thing." Now the truth came out. Not only was the dirt bag married, his wife was expecting a child! It got worse. The real reason for his reluctance to see me was his poor self-image. "You see, I am probably not anything like you think I am. I am in the worst shape I have ever been in," he admitted.

"Oh, John, don't be intimidated by me. My last fuck buddy was a hundred pounds overweight," I rationalized. "I just want to look in your eyes."

Having all this hot phone sex and anticipating getting laid had me horny, dripping wet, and out of control!

"The only thing I won't tolerate, John, is a two-inch pecker. I won't fuck a mushroom cap. You did tell the truth about your penis size, didn't you? It is six inches, isn't it?

"Five inches," he said.

"Five or three?" I questioned. I doubted his every word by now. John sounded nervous and scared and was obviously disappointed in himself.

He came up with the excuse that he could not come over tonight because he would never leave. Now the shit was really getting deep! John suggested that I meet him at his office.

"What should I wear?" I asked excited again.

"Anything!" John said, exasperated.

I was hoping he would at least request stockings and a garter belt, but it was getting late, and I thought better of it. I threw on some black jeans and put on my black boots and a red sweater over my white tank top. I was shaking with anticipation! When I arrived at the building, the automatic doors were locked. I tried to look inside and saw a figure moving in the hallway. I decided to go back to my car to get my cell phone to call John.

As I descended the steps, I heard John's voice calling after me. It was so dark I couldn't see him. I felt like an idiot.

"Where are you?" I asked. He was standing at a second set of doors farther down the walkway. In my mind, I was expecting John to look like his photo on the computer in spite of what he had told me—dark haired, broad shouldered, and wearing a suit. Instead, he had gray hair, a face much more weathered than his forty-nine years, and he had a large, lumpy upper body. We walked into his office together.

John was visibly scared to death! Now in the light, I got a better look. John was not wearing a suit like my fantasy man, but black pants, a red-and-blue windbreaker and black orthopedic-looking sneakers. I jumped into his arms and kissed him to relieve the awkwardness of the moment. John was trembling while kissing me passionately. The kiss wasn't bad at all.

Hot and frantic, John pulled off my sweater as I fumbled to unbutton his pants. I pulled his fly open to reveal giant white jockey underwear.

His cock was stiff and short, but adequate. John firmly grabbed me, then pulled up my shirt to fondle my big breasts. John attempted to undo my pants, but then we became tangled up with our pants at our knees and we both fell to the floor with our trousers at our ankles, wrapped around our shoes.

Oh God! I saw that John had doo-doo scratch marks on his underwear. I wondered at that moment how could men be so careless about details? Didn't he care about the impression he would make—and besides, didn't he want a clean crack anyway? I didn't mind a man a little rough around the edges, but not dirty! Gross!

The kissing, sucking, and fucking on the floor was all good, but his body was too large to comfortably get into a good rhythm.

At that moment, I realized that I had fucked too many fat men in my life and it was surreal that I was lying on an office floor bucking against Politician John's pelvic fat pad.

John was all hot and bothered and loosening up. He suggested that we go back to my house to continue the lovemaking. I made the excuse that I must go home alone at such a late hour. As we stood up to get dressed, I realized that John was severely pigeon-toed.

I returned home to my bedroom, numb and let down. John continued to call, and we had phone sex for a couple of years. I had hoped that he would eventually help me with the malpractice in my court case, but his efforts were lame at best. As time went on, I lost any respect I had for this John at all. It was high time to move on to my next adventure.

Twenty-Eight

THE BETRAYAL

When a person turns his or her back on someone, it could be taken as a reaction to an act, a knee-jerk type incident. In my life experience, it was quite different. Betrayal is an insidious, premeditated act driven by envy, coveting, hatred, and years of obsession and resentment. For a person to judge or control another to the point of hurt and harm and, on some occasions, loss of life, I believe is the most evil force of our human condition. What you are about to read is true; I am only one victim who survived to tell the tale of the ultimate betrayal of my life.

It was a September morning in 1997. I lay on a small table in my cosmetologist's house, receiving a milk-and-honey facial. I am a hard worker at any job I do, so pampering myself is not an option but a necessity of life. Vera was thirty minutes into the one-hour facial. I was deep into meditation, seeing only dark blue behind my closed eyelids, when I was flooded with a feeling of urgency and emotion. My grandmother's face came to me from the grave. She was anxiously telling me to call home. Something was wrong, and tears came to my eyes that I was desperately holding back so Vera wouldn't ask questions. I managed to get through the duration of the facial and left puzzled and confused, knowing my grandmother was trying to communicate something to me.

At the time, I had a pager and a cellular phone. Pagers had not become obsolete yet. When I got in my car, my pager had a 911 urgent message on it. It was from my younger sister.

Oh no! I thought; something terrible must have happened. My mind immediately went to my mother and father. I quickly called my sister.

"Deeanna, what has happened? Is someone hurt? Are Mom and Dad okay?" I asked.

"Persia, I just can't keep your secret anymore," Deeanna replied coldly. My mind had to readjust to comprehend what she said at first.

I shifted gears and asked, "Secret?"

"Yes, I am going to tell Mom and Dad that you are dancing at a strip club."

"Deeanna, why would you do that? They will only become concerned and worry themselves to death," I begged.

Before she started to ramble her distorted view of her rationalizations, I hung up. Stunned and numb, I realized now what my grandmother's ghost was warning me about.

I had to beat her to the punch. First, I called my mother. "Mom, I have to tell you something; I am dancing for a living now and not practicing nursing full-time anymore. Deeanna is going to call you and tell you. I want you to know that I am just fine and making money and working in a safe place."

"Why in the world would you tell Deeanna of all people? Why would you have not confided in me?" my mother asked, exasperated.

I was more than a little surprised at her question and her slur about Deeanna's character. She obviously knew more about this sister of mine than I did.

"I just didn't want you to worry and attach all the usual stereotypes to the profession. I told Deeanna because I was trying to convince her to go to medical school instead of nursing school, which I feel is a limited job for someone of her intelligence. She insisted that I was happy as a nurse, and if I was successful at nursing, then she wanted to do it too. I then confessed and told her I was so happy because I was dancing now."

Mom and I finished our conversation as I told her I had to call Dad before Deeanna got to him. My father was not as understanding.

"Hello, honey."

"Hi, Dad. I have something to tell you."

I could feel his right hand shaking back and forth. That is what he always does when he is upset.

"Dad, I am dancing now instead of nursing," I said poignantly.

"Who is dancing?" he demanded.

"I am!" I said.

"What kind of dancing?" he barked.

"Topless."

"So you lied to us!" he said.

"Dad, I am a single parent not receiving child support, and I am tired of the long, hard hours at the hospital."

Before he could start his tirade of verbal abuse, knocking me down as he always did, I used my easiest defense and hung up the phone. My body surged with adrenaline and disbelief at what had transpired from the time I woke up that morning until the present noon hour.

I thought to myself, the Sphos was right. She had warned me that everybody would eventually find out that I danced and use it against me. She used to say, "Nobody wants you to be happy. They want you to be miserable like they are in their boring, miserable lives."

The most irritating thing about my conversation with my father was his hypocrisy. Just in the past two years, he had been going to a local topless bar and dating dancers, giving them money and apartments. I had spent my childhood and adulthood battling an overprotective father who would not approve or validate anything I chose to do; even if I had been the prophet Muhammad reincarnated, he would have criticized me. I compounded my situation by marrying a weak, dependent husband who fought hard to keep me around. After all, I was the one who brought home the bacon.

I had reached a breaking point in my life, where I just wanted to be left alone to live my life the way I wanted to. My years as a stripper were by far the happiest and most fruitful of my life. I was able to do things that I never had done previously, like shop for things I wanted, save money, eat the food I wanted, and share these luxuries with my son. It was rewarding to provide private schooling for my son.

I saved every penny to put a down payment on a big, four-bedroom home that my son spent his elementary and middle-school years growing up in. The neighborhood we were living in was full of children, organized sports, and family activities.

My ex-husband never accepted invitations to visit his son in Florida, but instead spent a fortune on attorneys, attempting to get custody and child support from me! The battle waged from 1988 to 2000. He lost his first battle in 1990, when the judge who divorced us kicked him out for wanting custody of a child he refused to visit for two years. I had always encouraged the father to be a parent, but he was so scorned and self-centered that his anger toward me blinded him into an obsession of trying to control me. Our contact was consequently full of conflict and angst that would wax and wane, punctuated by months of silence.

Those times of no contact were peaceful and full of joy for my son and me. Otherwise, all contact was yet another threat of court, along with name-calling and verbal abuse from my ex-husband and his wife. I always abided by court law, which my ex continually ignored.

Confusion and abuse were all my son knew when he visited his father and stepmother. The stepmother would corner the boy and continually interrogate the child for information about me. "Who does she date? What kind of car does she drive? Where does she work?"

During this time my evil, meddling sister befriended my ex and his wife (not to my knowledge at the time). Her family was going to visit them and was aligning against me while manipulating my son by saying bad things about me in front of him. Her plan of turning our parents against me had failed, so as if she was some kind of metaphorical cartoon villain, she plotted another scheme to foil my happiness.

The most surprising element of this conflict was the fact that not once did we have an argument, ill thought, or confrontation growing up; on the contrary, she was nine years younger, and I was almost like a little mother to her. At one time, I had even approached my father to intervene after I discovered my sister was in horrible physical pain from treatment by a quack rheumatologist injecting her arthritic knees with cortisone multiple times. She confessed to me after I had read in my tarot cards that she was secretly crying in her pillow at night.

After I intervened with my father, she moved to be close to him, and he resolved her health problems under proper medical care. This sister had been diagnosed with rheumatoid arthritis at the age of two; consequently, our parents spoiled her and fretted over her illness, which created a cycle of self-pity and manipulation, compounding the disease rather than fostering mental health and well-being. I suppose this gave birth to her rotten and envious attitude toward me.

While visiting my mother in early 1998, my mother casually mentioned in a conversation that my evil sister had told my ex-husband about my new career and the fact that I had a soft-core website. My mother could not handle the smallest of confrontations. When she meekly told me this fact, my jaw dropped open in disbelief.

I exclaimed, "Deeanna told Alan I am a stripper?" My mother lowered her gaze in shame and told me that she had slapped her in the face upon learning this. Suddenly, I had a very satisfying visual of that moment, as I was familiar with a hard slap that my mother could deliver. At least Mom was on my side.

My dysfunctional family was draining my energy. I really just wanted to be left alone. I kept running in the other direction, hoping they would all just go away.

If I could turn the clock back, I would force them out with the aggression of a badger and have pursued Alan's responsibility as a father to pay the child support due to his son. In the interim, my attorney in Tennessee (which I had because it was the state in which Alan and I were divorced) had declared Florida as my son's home state. This protected him while my ex was on the warpath. To keep the story up to soap-opera standards, the judge who had granted our divorce had blown his brains out a couple of weeks before.

I may seem a little cuckoo to some, but for whatever reason, I have always been fascinated by the unknown and fantasy. I believe everybody has a sixth sense, and some are gifted and exercise it and develop the ability to use it. Over the years, I met and circumstantially was around "witches" or people who delved into the occult, the dark side and the lighter side. I am intrigued by the dark side, but not the least bit interested in any force that gives energy to darkness. I steer clear of books or cards like Alistair Crowley or any images that lean toward darkness. Tarot cards are a game and over the years I became proficient at reading the Rider-Waite deck.

With my experience, I have learned to respect the universe, have union with my faith in God, and I do not use the cards for earthly gain because it is impossible to do and an illusion at best. I also believe that one can objectively read cards for oneself, therefore, from time to time, I go to a card reader for fun, learning, and clarity, with emphasis on fun as a preteen schoolgirl may act when she wants to gossip with a friend about a crush she has on a boy in her class. The problem I always seem to encounter when I visit a psychic is remembering the questions I came to her for in the first place! I always draw a blank, just like I do when someone asks me what I would like for my birthday or Christmas. Any other day I could think of fifty things I would want! I learned to eventually take a list to the psychic, but that didn't seem to matter either.

On one particular day in 1998, I was inquiring about my new romance as people usually do, but the psychic kept focusing on my father in my cards. It annoyed me, as I hadn't even spoken to him in the past two years since he found out I was dancing.

"Why in the world was he in my cards?" I thought out loud.

The psychic consternated. "What are your father and ex-husband doing together?"

"What? Alan and Dad? They don't even like each other!" I exclaimed.

My psychic friend was flabbergasted and kept on. "I have never said this about anyone, but your father I would swear is the devil!"

I was really hoping for some good news about a soul mate romance that I could ride off into the sunset with on his white horse. Not to be. I just could not give my father or my ex any mental energy at that moment. I had finally liberated myself from the two men who had controlled me for all my life. I left the psychic's house unsatisfied and searching for answers on my own.

Years before in another city, I had visited a darker witch (not realizing it at the time). She was tall, slender, and blue eyed with dishwater-blond hair down to her waist. She did not wear any makeup and looked like a hippie chick with a maxi skirt and a peasant blouse. I could feel her power from across the room. I decided to tape the reading, but intuitively knew that the tape-recording would not be successful. When she started the reading, her tone was serious and her gaze one of concern. "You are a very kind person, and your family is wrong! You need to get as far away from your family as possible," she declared.

At the time, I was living in Naples, Florida, working at Lee Memorial Medical Center on a traveling nursing assignment. All my interactions with my family were warm and loving. I was fiercely independent and moved to a warmer climate to pursue golf and escape my groveling, alcoholic ex-husband whose drinking and laziness were killing me.

I couldn't comprehend what this woman was telling me. Over the years I learned that one thing a card reader cannot do is tell time. Whatever shows up in the cards that day may be correct, but the time line cannot be predicted.

Both women were accurate with their readings, but only to be seen many years later. As I left the dark witch, I was anxious to listen to the reading and process the surprising things she had told me, only to find a garbled and inaudible tape.

When my son turned twelve, I became concerned about his development. Up to this point, I had raised him alone financially, keeping him during the school year and sending him to his father to visit during the summers. I did not have a boyfriend during my dancing years, but had male "friends" around me that served as male role models for my son. I felt that young males need to be with their fathers during teenage years for fundamental development of their gender. I decided to call my ex-husband.

"Alan, I think it would be good for our son if he came to live with you during the school year and I keep him for the summer. Besides, I am really tired of being the disciplinarian and never having time to have fun or take a vacation with the boy!" I requested.

"Oh, I'll take him—only if you give me full custody and pay me child support," he demanded.

"Why should I pay you support when you have done nothing for our son monetarily or otherwise?" I asked.

"Persia, I know what you do!" he batted back.

"What are you saying?" I questioned.

"I know that you are a stripper!" Alan said.

I was surprised by this remark but continued the conversation without showing my emotion or breaking my cadence. "What does that have to do with me being a parent or this conversation right now?" I asked.

"I don't care that you dance, but I want custody and child support from you."

I slammed down the phone and broke into sobs, falling to pieces. I went into a rage. My evil sister's actions had hit me like a hammer to the head.

I grabbed a pair of scissors and with the help of my pseudo boyfriend, I cut the evil sister out of every family photo I had. Fat John would hand me a new photo album when I had finished butchering the one before. Since I had many family picture albums, this violent rage lasted about two hours. It was clear to me now how intertwined my sister had become with my ex-husband. The situation was so inappropriate and was becoming a sinister web in which all the actors involved were parasitic creatures attempting to devour me while using my son as a pawn in the success of their criminal plan.

My evil sister Deeanna became as obsessed with my dancing career and my website as my ex-husband had. She spewed her hatred and jealousy to my father, sister, ex-husband, and anyone else she could weave into her web of undoing. I just ignored all that I could and continued to stay close with my mother, who was torn between us. Despite her discomfort with being stuck in the middle of her children and their dilemma, she defended me to the end.

Enter Stalker John. Talk about fuel to a fire—this moron and con man I had married turned the situation into an inferno with a self-righteous vengeance. He wanted nothing less than to see me burn. Now I had two scorned lovers not only obsessing about me, but putting their heads together to bring me down.

I was in contact with my Tennessee attorney, who had been advising me well up to this point. I even contacted Broward County and got a case manager to try to collect back support from my ex-husband. In the meantime, the stalker ex had put my nude publications and my soft-core website in the hands of Alan and my father as a nice little package delivered to their homes very timely on Christmas Eve. From what I could gather, they couldn't stand this guy, but they used him for information about me. The stalker had lied and exaggerated, telling them I did webcam shows and had Johns visiting my house.

Alan's wife started leaving nasty messages on my machine with a string of ugly names, calling me a hooker. The stalker was also leaving messages, and one memorable one where he threatened my life.

"Your life is over as you know it now. I am going to kill you!" he claimed on my phone machine. I kept the recordings and used them as exhibits in court.

I hired a Florida attorney to assist with my case. He was a greedy fucker who put his lackey on my case while billing me top dollar. I wasn't an important enough person to give his professional attention to—he just wanted my sexual attention. The young Florida attorney was a sweet gal and worked hard for me.

To our surprise, my father ordered a police investigation of my home. It was a shocking blow! The black sheriff dropped by on three separate occasions, all surprise visits. Ironically, every time he came to the house, I was either preparing a meal fit for a king, had just had the house cleaned, or had been to the grocery store and had a refrigerator full of food. He must have thought I was Suzy Homemaker. The investigation was so invasive! The sheriff and his assistant went through my house with a fine-toothed comb, checking the computer and looking in every drawer in the house. They did not find the webcam they were told was operating or any sign of illegal activity. In fact, after the first visit, the sheriff took me outside and quietly said, "Hey, good luck with your website."

After the second visit, he started calling me several times a day asking me to go out with him. Thanks Daddy-O! What more could a daughter want from her father except more men hitting on her?

While the investigation was ongoing, my attorney asked me in a very serious tone, "Does your father want to kill you?"

I replied, "Good question; maybe he does!"

She was up in arms on how to proceed. The Tennessee court subpoenaed me to juvenile court after my ex-husband did not return my son to Florida after Christmas vacation. They even kept him out of school! He had contracted the flu while he was there and had a fever of 102 degrees.

Later, I found out that he had reached out to my father for family support to escape the verbal abuse from his stepmother. She was a Christian Scientist and did not believe in medication, so would not so much as give the boy a Tylenol for his fever.

All the villains were present and hovering over my poor son. The evil sister's husband, who happened to be a crash-course attorney, was a short, wormy guy with a pointed nose. He suggested and had my son sign an affidavit against me declaring me a prostitute and unfit mother.

I did hold one card: my ex-husband had declared in our first court case that I was "the best mother the boy could have." At that time, my conniving sister and brother-in-law were aligning themselves with my ex against me. My father got involved, and both my father and ex-husband were showing my soft-core website (at the time) while the stalker ex-husband was feeding them lies the entire time.

I flew to Tennessee in February of 2000 to juvenile court. My father, sister, brother-in-law, ex-husband, and his wife were all in the courtroom.

They had hired an older attorney who appeared very uncomfortable when he saw me alone against the group. The judge listened to both sides, and when my father and ex confessed to exposing the boy to my website, he berated them and said, "It seems to me that you are the party damaging the child. I will take the child alone in my chambers now."

After forty-five minutes with our son, he returned and stated, "This boy clearly belongs with his mother and will return home to Florida immediately." He adjourned the court and left. I rose to walk out with my attorney, and my ex-husband's wife brushed her shoulder into mine. With adrenaline naturally surging through my veins, this was all I needed to shove her across the pew ready to pull all her hair out. My father then yelled, "You shouldn't be doing that to your son!"

I yelled back, "You are nothing but a lowly snake, old man!"

My attorney had me by the arm and hurried me out. Their attorney dismissed himself from their service.

Our son was sent home, very angry and confused. He was behind in school, and my working schedule compounded the problem. I was working like a slave to keep up with paying the bills and attorney fees. My ex had even stooped to calling the Christian school I had our boy attending and telling the principal that I was a stripper! All his actions caused our son grief and did not accomplish anything else.

Things got worse. The enemy proceeded to a higher court and took the case to the Fourth Circuit Court of Judge Milicent Robertson. My father hired her relative, Paul Robertson, as the attorney to represent my ex-husband. News of this actually pleased me, as this judge was notorious for destroying deadbeat Dads.

The hurt and the pain from this betrayal were unconscionable. My own father was paying to sue his own daughter! He had never offered to help us financially or otherwise. Even more maddening was the fact that my ex was as tight as a clam's ass and would steal funds from his own children, which in fact he was doing! My Florida attorney was as stunned as I was. Her senior partner was of no assistance except to send invoices to me punctually.

I had total trust in my Tennessee attorney at this point, but having to pay out so much money left me searching for answers, and the constant expenses seemed to cloud any progress toward justice. My meek, sweet mother was steady and as supportive as she could be. Non-confrontational and a subject of rejection from her other daughters put us in a tailspin. In the midst of all the chaos, I was being stalked by the moron I had married and divorced the year before.

My Florida attorney had become very frustrated with the Tennessee attorney. He wouldn't return calls or answer simple questions. I was getting mixed feelings about him when he told me we needed character witnesses and started getting my friends and neighbors involved in the case. It seemed unnecessary, and it was embarrassing to have my dirty laundry aired because of my ex-husband's vendetta! My Florida attorney and I were out of answers. The court date was set for June, once again in Tennessee.

Judge Millicent Robertson was notorious for intolerance for deadbeat fathers. I was looking forward to being in a court with an honest judge who could give me a reprieve from my hostile ex-husband. Millicent Robertson had delicate, weak features, a coiffed hairdo of a kind of a sixties bob; her makeup was modest, but she went overboard when she put on her lip liner this morning. I have only been to the circus a couple of times in my life. I never cared for them. The clowns were scary and carnival people all creepy and the animals seemed angry and not having any fun. Well, I had just thought I had been to a circus, but in reality I hadn't until I entered the Fourth Circuit Court of Millicent Robertson's courtroom. This was where the real circus was performed—a real live kangaroo court it was!

The deal had been made and done way ahead of time. Nepotism at is best! The court had become a pathological mire where a judge usurped her power to write law for egotistical advancement. My son was the innocent soul who inevitably would pay the price.

My mother, son, and Fat John boyfriend flew to Nashville to appear in court. We were face to face with the enemy outside the courtroom: my father, his wife, her youngest daughter (ten years old), my half-sister (nine years old), my evil, jealous sister, her husband, my ex-husband, his wife, and the biggest shocker, my religious, Bible-thumping sister from St. Louis, who was standing there, chatting it up with my ex-husband's wife. When my son saw the group, his only comment was, "I can't believe *she* came!" referring to the religious sister. Like me, he fully expected this kind of behavior from the rest of the bunch, but the religious sister had always kept her distance and minded her own business—done the Christ-like thing, if you will.

My mother was exasperated and commented on how surreal the whole thing was. I was standing there, numbly waiting for someone to come up with a branding iron to apply a big scarlet letter to my chest with before burning me alive at the stake!

My son, mother, and I sat facing the court in the next-to-the-last pew. It was a large courtroom, with about twenty rows of seating. The case being heard when court began was a woman who had been a defense attorney in Tennessee. She was attempting to save her marriage of two years to her slimy cop husband, who had been cheating on her via an Internet relationship. He wanted a divorce and all her money.

She was a very attractive blonde and was lucky enough to be educated and familiar with the Fourth Circuit Court and their procedures; unfortunately, she wasn't savvy enough to work this judge. The woman's husband took the stand to be nothing more than what he was—a liar, a cheat, and a thief! The wife expressed to the judge that in spite of his infidelity, she wanted to save the marriage. What happened next made my jaw drop open and knocked the air out of my lungs.

The judge retorted, "Well, he obviously does not want to be married to you! You are to pay him forty thousand dollars over the next six months by this court's orders. Court adjourned."

My case was the next one on the docket. The judge glanced at it, balked, and decided to hear it in the morning. Mind you, it was only

10:00 a.m., and she was aware that my son and I had traveled from Florida.

We were all dismissed. I encountered the poor blonde victim of the court in the ladies' restroom. She was sobbing profusely, telling me that the money she was to pay her husband was her inheritance from her father, which he had just left her. They had been married only two years and did not have any children. What I had just witnessed was extortion by an evil judge who had become so self-absorbed over the years that she had morphed into a salivating, bottom-feeding creature that survived on brutality and torture of people for her own false sense of power. She was rotten from the inside out, and the worst of it was that I had to face her the next day.

The feelings of loss and doom were daunting, and I was just another victim who had to endure the undoing of a life I had worked so hard to create for my beautiful son and myself. It was unbelievable being with my family and leaving the courthouse with the eyes of the other half of my family watching our every movement as we left the building.

Here we were, a family that had grown up together in middle America, my father clambering up the ladder of success through medical school with my mother supporting him every step of the way. We had family dinners every night and special ones on Sundays. My father traditionally cooked french toast on Saturday mornings. We started out in a small suburb in Oklahoma City, then moved to Seattle, Washington, where my father completed his fellowship. In 1968, we moved to a beautiful neighborhood in Memphis, Tennessee, to a house on a lake.

It was the year 2000 now, and I had to hold my head high with a choking sensation in my throat and the pit of my stomach feeling like a knotted rope. I had to push the memories aside and face the dark reality of the day.

My mother's face mirrored the shock and hurt we all felt. My son, just twelve years old, had the look of any child who had just been slapped in the face by the people who had told him they loved him. It was maximum confusion that the human mind just could not untangle.

We spent most of our day distracting ourselves with the beauty of our hotel: Union Station in downtown Nashville. The hotel had been a train station that was converted into a hotel. It was like being in a brass-and-glass bubble in a conservatory. The rooms had elegant furnishings with gold and velvet fabrics and accessories. It was a comfortable place to stay, but the events ahead left us all with an unspoken anticipation that overwhelmed any physical beauty or comfort we were experiencing at that moment.

Then next morning, I felt as if I were going to my own execution. A therapist I used to visit from 1989 to 1992 came to mind. She told me once that she had never met anyone who could hold back emotion like I could. She taught me how to cry. Today, I was not that girl who learned to cry. I was tough and strong and ready for battle—and a battle it was!

As people will do, we sat in the same places as we had the day before. Only my son, ex-husband, and I were allowed in the courtroom. Before entering, my mother jokingly showed me the name of her lipstick that she was wearing. As she turned the tube upside down, we both read the name: Karma.

My son and I both noticed my wormy brother-in-law jumping up and down, peering through the small, square-cut glass window of the courtroom door. He was an attorney, one of the guys who had to take the bar exam several times to pass and got into law because he was a busybody, not because he was a humanitarian or solid citizen. He was a very short man with a Napoleon complex. I just hated him for his involvement in this mess. We had probably only had a couple of conversations between ourselves, and his meddling was unraveling my family. Since my father and my evil sister were testifying against me, they would have their time on the stand.

The case was opened, and both attorneys were presenting their opening statements. My son looked at me wide-eyed, questioning me about our attorney. "Mom! He isn't saying anything!"

It was obvious to me that he had to kowtow to this judge. He was protecting his ass; after all, he had to face this cunt on a regular basis.

He lamely took a seat next to me as I sat there numb in my black skirt and white blouse.

Then next morning, I felt as if I were going to my own execution. him for his involvement in this mess. We had probably only had a couple of conversations between ourselves, and his meddling was unraveling my family. Since my father and my evil sister were testifying against me, they would have their time on the stand.

He lamely took a seat next to me as I sat there numb in my black skirt and white blouse. The defense went for my throat and aggressively attempted to defame my character, but not before my ex-husband pathetically kept inserting his foot in his mouth, to the point that his attorney finally told him to shut up. His attorney's aunt, the judge—oh yes, they were related—asked sarcastically, "Do you let your counselor talk to you that way?"

My ex looked angry, hurt, and nauseous. I saw the pain in his eyes when he looked at me. He had never stopped loving me, and the scorn he carried was like a tattoo on his eyeballs. Attorney Robertson wasn't about to let his client on the stand. Their case was built on a pack of lies, and my ex was a terrible liar who had come to court thinking that the court was a benevolent body that would take the side of his self-centered, pathetic ass. He did not get the last laugh.

My father took the stand and verbally disapproved of my lifestyle as a dancer and felt that it was better for my son to live with my ex-husband—although this man had never visited his grandson in Florida or participated in our lives at all. He and my sister both cried on the stand, expressing their love for me. It took all my willpower not to stand up and scream "fuck you!" to both of them. At that moment, I was so embarrassed to be related to these two people.

It was my turn now. Everybody, with the exception of my ex-husband and my son, was just relishing in the circus that had been created here today. All the bailiffs and staff from the other courts came to watch.

It was like a public stoning or beheading. I was waiting for the crowd to start chanting, "Guillotine!"

Mr. Robertson introduced my recent catastrophic marriage to Stalker John, who had told my ex and my father that I was a prostitute who had all kinds of wild activities in my house and even had cameras set up for the Internet. The enemy had held an investigation of my house on two occasions, surprise visits from the local sheriff each time. Both times, the searches had come up negative. At this point, my attorney introduced Exhibit A, presenting my tape recording of a phone message of Stalker John threatening me, saying, "Your life is over as you know it today!"

Mr. Robertson stopped the tape abruptly and dismissed any further testimony by Stalker John. Next, he pulled out his second weapon, my website: www.persiaspalace.com. He had all eighty-seven galleries of soft, girl-girl, nude photos downloaded from the Internet. I was laughing on the inside. This stupid asshole was trying to embarrass me!

"Is this you?" he would ask as he would display a nude picture of me. Without blinking, I would answer yes over and over and over with each photograph.

Mr. Robertson's stare was blank and cast downward at the floor. I could tell he was calculating, and I watched him ease into plan C.

"In this home video, what was this simulated ejaculation you did made of?"

"Vanilla pudding and piña colada yogurt!" I confidently entertained. A chuckle from the mob arose. He still couldn't get so much as a blink out of me. He moved onto plan D. He whipped out the *Gent* magazine issue of August 1999 with photos of me in the home body section. The photos were one of Guido's famous shoots where I was spread eagle, pinching my nipples in the back of a stretch limo. Mr. Robertson handed the magazine to his cousin or aunt or however this corrupt judge was he was related to. She sharply asked, "What are you doing in this picture?"

"Well, your honor, I was celebrating my birthday," I answered.

"Is this how you celebrate your birthday?" she questioned.

Almost deadpan, I paused and replied, "Well, not every year."

The spectacle continued for two more hours. The judge attempted to question my cash business, trying to expose any tax evasion. She tried to expose inappropriate behavior I might have had with the boyfriend (Fat John), my mother, and my child in hotel room we were staying in while we were in Nashville on this visit. I proceeded to ask the judge if families pitch separate tents when they go camping and continued explaining that we do not get undressed in each other's presence and carry on as any normal family does when traveling.

When I was finally dismissed from the stand, my attorney leaned over and said, "You sounded very honest up there."

I looked at him with surprise and disdain, exclaiming, "That is because I am honest."

On the other side, my ex had perjured his statement, lying on his mortgage loan application, stating he was obligated to zero dollars in child support among other things. The court overlooked that. My attorney did not call my mother to the stand, only my obese boyfriend, who was a champion telling the court that he was the man at my son's ball games and piano recitals, not the father. It didn't matter; the court used his statement as a man who slept with a woman out of wedlock. The judge then took our son into her chambers. It was brief, maybe ten minutes, and I felt inside that her words were probably manipulative and abusive.

The court had made its decision: The father shall be granted custody, receiving $620 in child support each month. The mother will have visitation on designated holidays and during the summer vacation, and transportation costs will be divided. The mother is forbidden to have single men at her house.

The mob gasped! In seconds, my son screamed out loud and burst into tears. My ex-husband and I locked eyes, and I saw regret, remorse, and pain—not victory or revenge. I think he was the most shocked at the verdict. The judge satisfied her purpose, to write case law in Tennessee. The judge then yelled out, "Who has let the child in the courtroom?"

I thought to myself, Doesn't the bitch have control over her own courtroom? My boyfriend looked coolly at me and said, "She is going to rot in hell for this."

I was in shock. My son was crying profusely. I was numb, shut down, and I almost could not respond to my son's cries, but he needed me to cry with him at the moment, so I did. My attorney was physically separating us and handing him over to the opposing party, who began to huddle around him. They would not even let him change his clothing. He was wearing very uncomfortable dress shoes. I was living a nightmare!

My mother had disgust, hatred, and rage all over her face. To think I had given my greedy attorney another thousand dollars that morning! He knew he was going to throw the case. It was cold blooded, barbaric, and really bad karma. My boyfriend and I said our good-byes to my mother, who had to drive back to Memphis. I put on my son's gold plaid shirt, which was the only belonging he had left in his car, and went to the Nashville airport to return to our home in Florida.

I got wrecked on dirty martinis in the airport lounge. Swollen and numb from crying, all I could do was try not to think about the separation so much. My son had it much worse. He would become his stepmother's houseboy over the next five years. His father was an alcoholic with the spine of a jellyfish and allowed his battle-ax wife to steamroll everyone. She was a dyed-in-the-wool vegan, right down to baking beet birthday cakes for her one-year-old daughter. My ex and his wife did not send our son to school but homeschooled him in a non-accredited program. The mean old bitch would wake our son up every morning at six to do housework. She would throw away his clothes if she didn't like them and constantly said bad things about me, calling me names. The poor dear used to call me after midnight from under his bedcovers, whispering to me about wanting to run away. I warned him that once they received the phone bill, our late-night talks would end. The five years apart were painful, tedious, and full of drama.

My only consolation was that our son would see the real man his father was and at least would have spent some years living with him, no matter if he was an unfit parent in my eyes. Any male role model is better than none, in my opinion. Yes, this was an interlude where our son would be put to the test while his father and stepmother obsessed on my lifestyle and bombarded the boy with a stream of hostile, judgmental, and stereotypical, verbal vomit about his mother. Does child abuse come in a more damaging form?

Twenty-Nine

MONTEL WILLIAMS

Life is full of wonderful surprises: new relationships, weddings, a baby's birth, divorces, illness, and all the things that make a life a full one. But the ones that are unexpected are probably the most exciting to experience and celebrate—for example, getting that phone call from Publishers Clearing House (do those people really exist?) or realizing you have the winning lotto ticket.

Well, my phone call came in mid-July 2001. I was in Fargo, North Dakota, playing in a golf tournament. What a godforsaken place! If I had seen the movie *Fargo* before I went there, I would have never gone. That town is haunted! Anyway, I was fortunate to get to play in this golf tournament, but had four miserable days between toe hooks off every tee and those goddamn biting flies.

While I was in my dingy hotel room, I thought I might as well check my phone messages from my landline. I had received a phone call from the *Montel Williams Show*, in reference to my custody battle in Tennessee. They wanted me to appear on the show the following week!

The media vulture from the *Tennessean* newspaper had done me a favor. He had been lurking in the Nashville courtrooms, preying on people's dirty laundry, and written an article that caught the eye of a few producers. Once the story hit the newspapers and the Internet, I had reached out to the National Organization for Women, Oprah Winfrey, and various other personalities. Court TV had called me several times wanting a *Jerry Springer*–type scene with other family members on their show. I refused to feed those lions.

The *Montel Williams* staff had a more professional and much different approach. It felt right. I'd had nine months to absorb the loss of my son, the shock, pain and betrayal from my family, and our "just us" system we have in the court system of the United States. Finally I had a chance to tell my side of this family fiasco!

Everything was right on time!

The staff had my room booked at the Helmsley on Second Avenue and had a twenty-five-dollar-a-day spending allowance for me. They would arrive in the morning to pick me up for the show. I unpacked and decided to pay *Cheri* magazine a visit in my spare time. They had misprinted me in my 1999 publication, putting my photo and bio next to another slut. I wanted to set them straight.

I went downstairs and hailed a cab, asking the driver to take me to 801 Second Avenue. He turned the corner and took me a hundred feet and stopped. Thinking he was being a wise guy, I asked him, "What are you doing?" He said, "This is Second Avenue." What a dick! I let him keep the money and had to laugh at myself for being so stupid.

I flounced down the street to the building and went up to the ninth floor of the skyscraper. The receptionist was butt ugly (guess she wasn't overpaid), but she managed to get me through the door to meet the associate editor. I had talked with him a few times on the phone and expected to meet a middle-aged, heavyset, salt-and-pepper-haired man—wrong! Much to my surprise, a young, lanky blond fellow with a nice smile invited me into his office. I kindly showed him and his colleague the error they had made in printing with bios and unmatched photos. They both told me that they would definitely reprint me and for me to send them recent photos. Both men were in a behind-the-scenes shop and told me they had never met anyone they had published.

I had dinner with one of my Johns, a longtime customer from the club who happened to be a stockbroker. Over the years, I kept him from getting taken by strippers and whores, and he gave me good advice in general about life. I was glad to hear he was finally getting laid and possibly married soon. Champagne, laughter, and a little bit of hanky-panky made the night complete.

I was up at 6:30 a.m., starting to get nervous about the show. What if I got stage fright? My concierge was late, and I was getting peeved. I started thinking "Fuck! I could have had breakfast and an extra hour of sleep."

Another victim to appear on the show was in the lobby: a strawberry blonde wearing a bright-blue polyester suit. She had lost her government job because she and her husband had launched a website with the two of them having some adult fun, and a coworker saw it and reported it to her boss. She had appeared on other shows and was a fill-in for a no-show, trailer-trash skank who couldn't show up for whatever reason.

Goddamn it! I was getting nervous sitting in the green room, waiting to appear on the show. No script, no preparation—just throw-you-to-the-wolves orientation. I looked down at my hands. They were cold and clammy without any veins in sight. All my blood was in my stomach. This was much worse than first-tee jitters or the very first day of school when I was five years old.

The other girls on the show were just as nervous, and I taught them about yoga breathing while we were in the wings waiting to go on. One of the girls had a scholarship for track and field and was stripping for extra money. The school got wind of this, and she lost her position on the track team and made headline news. Once we all got on the set and were seated, I stopped sweating quite as much.

Montel was great! He was a talented man with the gift of gab! He could certainly get the rhythm and conversation flowing. In fact, it was really hard to get a word in edgewise or answer in questions the audience might have.

Montel introduced me and gave a brief statement about my nursing career and that I was now dancing topless to support my son and myself and touched on the fact that I lost custody due to my choice of profession. When he asked me what happened, I told him that I gave up being a health-care provider to be an adult entertainer provider. Montel jumped on that and repeated my statement, resonating very loudly: adult entertainment provider.

When Montel asked me what happened in the courtroom, I said, "Well, Montel, the judge's nephew was my ex-husband's attorney, so it was pretty much a done deal, wouldn't you say?"

Montel did not respond to that statement, and subsequently, that was edited out of the program. Obviously, even talk show hosts have to kiss ass to the politicians to stay alive. The young track star on the panel was very meek, the other woman was kind of old news, and the focus was mainly on her attorney defending her First Amendment rights. I was asked the most questions, with about 30 percent support from the audience and the other 70 percent attacking me verbally.

Naturally, hindsight is twenty-twenty when one is asked questions spontaneously. I answered four hostile members of the audience. My best response was to a young woman who asked me how I could leave the noble profession of nursing, where I could help so many people in exchange for being in a place like a topless bar with all the scum and drugs.

I proceeded to tell her the story from the first chapter of this book when I saved the dancer in the club. "Let me tell you something: the first week I danced, a girl had a respiratory arrest in the dressing room, and I saved her life. If I had not been there, she most likely would have died. Maybe I was supposed to be there for that reason alone." She had nothing to say in response to that!

Another angry woman yelled out at me: "I have a one year old at home, and I can't imagine leaving him at home to go dance in a topless bar."

My response to her attack was lame, but afterward I thought of the perfect comeback: "If you have a one-year-old baby at home, lady, then what in the world are you doing in the audience of a talk show bashing a stripper?"

Prologue: Doomsday

It was a sunny September morning in south Florida. I woke up around 7:30 a.m. to get my VCR hooked up to the television to record the *Montel Williams* episode I was to appear on. As my friend and I were trying to get all the connections secure, we watched a plane fly into the World Trade Center in New York City. We were both stunned and wondered for a moment if this was really happening. It was so surreal that it seemed like some kind of sick joke. Then, just minutes later, another plane flew into the second building!

It was my big day to get my story heard on national television, and right in front of my eyes, I felt like the world was coming to an end. I was ashamed inside for thinking my life had any significance at all at that moment. I sank to my knees, with my eyes transfixed on the screen and horrific scene exploding in New York City. The phone rang and my mother called to tell me that she was watching me on the *Montel Williams* show and that her sister was in Oklahoma was watching it too! I told her about the planes flying into the World Trade Center and that I wouldn't be watching the show, and for her to change the channel to see what was happening in our indivisible United States.

September 12, 2001

I woke up at 5:30 a.m. the next morning gasping. For the first time in my forty-three years, I was scared. The World Trade Center had been destroyed and did not exist today. Thousands had died, many jumping to their deaths to escape the inferno of the burning towers. The reality had hit me, and it was not a nightmare that would go away. I felt vulnerable and unsafe and started to think about all the things I hadn't done in my life and all the experiences I still wanted. It was excruciatingly painful that I could not be with my son and hold him in my arms at that moment.

My mind went back in time to when our elementary school showed mandatory films on nuclear war and radioactive fallout and how people would live underground. Every Saturday at noon, the city would sound the war sirens, and it was an ominous reminder of the possibility of nuclear war and living in a basement with strangers away from the sunlight so the fallout wouldn't eat our skin away. I am not sure what year the sirens stopped blaring at lunchtime; I must have been in my teens.

I thought about all those years in school when we said the Pledge of Allegiance every morning and in fifth grade when my homeroom teacher conducted the class to sing "God Bless America" with such jubilation.

This morning I was confused and trying to sort all of the prior day's events out in my brain. It felt like Judgment Day in one of those movies. Maybe Nostradamus was right after in all his predictions. Or maybe this was all a conspiracy of evil and power.

I started recalling all the precious moments I had had with my son and then I thought about all the families who lost their loved ones the day before. I am so grateful that I learned to live in the moment. There was no tomorrow for the thousands who died on September 11, 2001.

Ode to Persia

Once in a lifetime comes a woman so fair, all worries

leave, and so does care.

With eyes of brown and hair in a mane, she will most

certainly drive you insane.

Of generous bosom and yet so smart, you must lay your

head to her heart.

Who is this lass who gathers such praise? Persia, of

course, as we stand in amaze. Long arms and legs we

love so much—many a yearning man pines to touch.

Certainly a sweet mouth with great talent, a tongue to

match, much wasted if I haven't.

Smooth dark skin flowing over curves. Aroma quite nice if

memory serves.

A tongue unmatched and she can swallow—oh yes, a

woman we will always follow.

Hands that know how and where to touch…sometimes it

is all just too much.

My staff in hand and in salute—

if she would only but play the flute. My plain heart is

spread open wide; in vain I hope she goes inside. If only

to hold and yea to keep her,

to end a quest that longs to seek her.

Worry not if her short stay has such intensity. The memo-

ries will surely last for all eternity.

/

Thirty

Life after *Montel*

During a crisis, people express their sympathy, shock and approval or disapproval, pat you on the back, and life moves on. Without my son I felt numb, but to carry on, I blocked the painful thoughts as best I could. The entire court scene was so surreal that I could not comprehend it as reality. Work was therapy, and I worked harder than ever during those years.

My son wanted to run away from his court-appointed home. He had literally become his stepmother's houseboy. Up at 6:00 a.m. most days, homeschooled and forced to eat a vegan diet at thirteen years old. His alcoholic father was busy pouring his woes into a beer can starting at 2:00 p.m. every day.

The boy desperately wanted to escape from his vindictive stepmother. He would call me at late hours in the night from under his bedcovers telling me how he wanted to run away. I told him that because of the court order, my hands were tied and that I would be kidnapping him if I helped him get away. It was just a matter of time before they received the phone bills and took the phone out of his room.

The new family never honored the visitation ordered by the court, so I was forced to sue to enforce getting to see my son for one holiday. It was a hassle and emotionally taxing for everyone.

We endured five years of the usual manipulation that goes on between broken families—and a little extra with the wicked stepmother calling me names on the phone and refusing to let my son and I talk to each other. My ex-husband was never capable of an adult conversation, and as much as I tried to communicate with him, there was always an impasse or dead end.

The day the boy turned eighteen, he was finally able to be free of the court order and boarded a plane to Florida not a day later. You see, the child-support checks had ceased—no more gravy train, and the pawn son was of no use to the father. The boy looked like a prisoner of war when he arrived at his Florida home. His ribs showed, and he was mentally exhausted. For the first two months, he slept long hours and quickly resumed his normal weight.

Since the custodial parents didn't bother to put the boy in an accredited high school, but chose to homeschool him without having the education or credentials to do so, the prepaid college fund I had provided for him since he was three years old was of no use, as colleges wouldn't accept him. A private university was his only option. Thanks to our forefathers, the son accumulated huge student loans to help pay for his education.

I am so lucky to have my son, and I believe he feels the same way about me. We have life, health, happiness, and many talents. In the face of such a dysfunctional family, we survived and managed a functional life together.

Thirty-One

The Unintended Fuck You

During our five years apart, I escaped Florida and lived in Mexico for a couple of years. It was a fun place to run to, and culturally it was an excellent education to a third world society. It was my first time I lived in a country without a middle class. The Aztec Mexicans were sweet, hardworking people, short in stature and thick and sturdy.

The climate was hot and tropical—very relaxed, unless one challenged the local politics. Then you entered the twilight zone where gringas and gringos are pushed to the fringes, where the locals wanted them to be in a foreign land. Americans take so many conveniences for granted. The quality of water in Mexico is so poor; my hair became dry and brittle, and I longed for a luxurious hot bath. So many days only cold showers were available.

I had many people suggest for years that I turn my website from a soft-core site to hard core. Since Judge Robertson condemned me as a stripper, I was plenty angry and had nothing to lose at this point. My father was going to teach me a lesson with his vindication; ironically, because of his action, his worst fears became a reality, and I became a pornographer and film star.

I decided to turn to the adult industry, and PersiasPalace.com went hard core. Getting into the film industry was one of the best things I ever did. I just wish I had done it in the late nineties! I started to film my own movies in 2003. I partnered with a guy in Florida who ran the website while I found talent and did the production end of it. He ended up being lazy, so we parted ways after six months.

I would travel to Florida and continued to dance in the clubs. I just loved the club scene and dancing and everything that comes with it: the costumes, the music, the smell of liquor mixed with cigarettes, and the neon lights, the beautiful women, and even the overbearing DJ's and managers.

Unfortunately for me, the days of wishing I could drink vodka all day like the other dancers were upon me. I had inherited the genetics of my mother, and the progression of alcoholism had become a monkey on my back. The adage "Be careful what you wish for" was very true in my life with my drinking problem. Blackouts and angry drunkenness put an end to my dancing days.

Realizing there was nothing in Mexico for me, I moved back to Florida in 2005. I made a feeble attempt at working in real estate. It was so boring compared to my bar life. I continued to dance and decided with the exposure of the *Montel* show and the public embarrassment of the court case, why not use my stage image to grow it in the film industry? Promote it I did indeed! The self-destructive bar scene was just what I needed to get into the next phase.

I started working on my website with a vengeance. I went to all the adult industry seminars and conventions to learn about the business. I was impressed how many "normal" people were making a good living in the adult industry. It was surprising and calming to meet people who had a matter-of-fact attitude about the industry. Being around them, the social stigma of not being taken seriously melted away.

I have always been a sexual creature and have been a free spirit, not caring about the pressures in society, but deep inside the lack of family support would haunt me once in a while. I kept on track, however, and soon became a sexpert. I started shooting for other companies to build a stronger brand and assumed the name Persia Monir as my porn-star personality. So many men dominated the business; I could not grasp how affiliate programs worked and how some of the websites accumulated large sums of money. I just continued to put myself out there and tried to learn from as many people as I could. I found a couple of people to work with who were solid, honest, and trustworthy (which is hard to find in any line of work). Since any adult business has been associated with organized crime and nefarious characters; it has never been legitimized legally by our members of Congress. The film industry was strongly intertwined with the economy in California. Location rental and everything else that goes with filming—makeup artists, costumes, models and talent, and traveling—all pumped money back into the local cities. The business thrived until the crash of 2008.

A handful of entrepreneurs created tube sites. Through advertising and ripping off everyone's intellectual content, the tube sites became a leviathan of a network. I called it the modern-day "blob." Baffled and stuck, the expert panels at the adult seminars put their heads together on how to control the tube sites. Without knowing it, the takeover had already consumed the Internet and the public porn for free had saturated the market. The adult market had been pirated, and the industry as we knew it became a sinking ship. It was so much fun, and it was sad seeing the business change and not having any control over it. I remember shooting a scene in LA with a co-actress watching the scene. She had decided to only shoot mainstream film but told me she really missed the adult filming industry and that it was so much more fun. It really was like shooting comedy so much of the time. Sex is fun, and creating it on film is a blast, literally! After shooting two of my own films, I produced my last film in 2011. It had become a cool thing for young amateur women and men to suck off boyfriends online for kicks. The entire scene lost all its sex appeal (if it ever had any in the first place) and just became lewd, common, and mundane.

Thirty-Two

THE HAPPY ENDING

The *Book of Johns* would be incomplete without a happy demise, right? If human beings were able to see their own futures or destinies, they would more than likely try to change the events or act differently in one's own present situation or time in life.

This is the predicament with reading tarot cards or consulting psychics; it is frowned on by those who rely on faith in "God" and trust in a Higher Power. Personally, I have used both trains of thought interchangeably in my life. For the record, I for one can't handle knowing the future. Anytime my fortune has been read, whether I was doing it for fun or happened upon a psychic person by chance, I came to expect the change in my life on my schedule, when I wanted it, not when the Universe was to present change in my life.

Experience has taught me that psychics cannot tell time. They may be able to see into the future, but it may be immediate or years from now. Not once, but at least a half a dozen times, psychics, card readers, witches, and wiccans that I have met predicted a light-haired, light-eyed man coming into my life. It would go like this:

"He is so kind, so smart, an excellent business man!"

"It will be love at first sight!"

"You will travel the world with this man, and he will make all of your dreams come true! You will meet him in your middle age. He has sandy-colored hair and very light eyes."

"This man is so strong, so gentle, I see lots of white hair; he is older. I have never seen cards this good for anybody!"

The older man part used to bother me. I was anything but a gold digger. I wanted love before anything and a natural relationship, which happens with someone around the same age mostly. The first prediction was around the year 1990. Another one came in 1997 and then yet another in 2002. I think one psychic was trying to predict the month and time and insisted he was all over my cards and very close to me physically, where I was living. I was becoming impatient and starting to feel like maybe these people were seeing into my next lifetime.

Now, I know this sounds like it can't be true, but listen to what happened next. I went to Rome in September 2011. I was there with a man I had a fling with who, by the way, did not have light eyes or hair! The vacation was cut short in Venice. I left the asshole and went to Rome on my own.

While there, I was taking a tour of the Vatican and met a lady who I ended up having dinner with that evening. Coincidentally (no pun intended), we dined next to the Trevi fountain, the fountain that the movie *Three Coins in the Fountain* was based on. I decided to try my luck, and with three coins in my right hand, I threw them over my left shoulder wishing for Prince Charming with the light hair and light eyes to come into my life.

As destiny was predicted, on November 19, 2011, he walked into my life. The first time I gazed into those baby-blue eyes, I knew he was the one. A golden boy he was. Everything those witchy women said about him was spot-on: good-looking, successful, smart, a great businessman, a father, funny, sexy, social, a real live dream man.

What else could a woman want in a man? Well, I will tell you, not only is he all those things, he is strong enough to handle an independent woman with a crazy past and a very sexual life. He is the only man I have ever met who can handle me and be supportive and loving.

Good riddance to all the misogynist men in my past.

So I got my happy ending—and as for the cards, I don't care to read them or hear any predictions. Life is just fine the way it is without knowing.

Made in the USA
Middletown, DE
06 November 2018